I0023346

Joseph B. Killebrew

Meadows and Pastures

A compendium of the grasses of Tennessee, prepared expressly for the

farmers of Tennessee, but adapted to the whole country

Joseph B. Killebrew

Meadows and Pastures
A compendium of the grasses of Tennessee, prepared expressly for the farmers of Tennessee, but adapted to the whole country

ISBN/EAN: 9783337227111

Printed in Europe, USA, Canada, Australia, Japan

Cover: Foto ©Andreas Hilbeck / pixelio.de

More available books at **www.hansebooks.com**

MEADOWS & PASTURES.

A Compendium of the

GRASSES OF TENNESSEE,

PREPARED EXPRESSLY FOR THE

FARMERS OF TENNESSEE,

But Adapted to the Whole Country.

By J. B. KILLEBREW, A. M., Ph. D.,

Published by the Bureau of Agriculture, Statistics and Mines, for the State of Tennessee.

NASHVILLE:
ALBERT B. TAVEL, PRINTER TO THE STATE.
1883.

INTRODUCTION.

No surer test of the degree of agricultural advancement of a country can be found than the relative acreage of land laid down to grass and devoted to tillage. Wherever the grass is most abundant there is the highest farming. This statement is most strikingly established by comparing the agricultural systems of France and England. In France 53 per cent of the tillable land is annually sown in some kind of grain, while in England the grain-bearing per cent of land is only 25. On the other hand, while France has but 22 per cent in grass, England has 50. Notwithstanding this difference in the amount of land devoted to grain, the yield of wheat to each inhabitant is almost identical in the two countries Every acre of grain land in England receives, on an average, the manure from the animals fed off three acres of grass. In France, on the contrary, the manure made from each acre of grass has to be spread over two and a half acres of grain. In other words, each acre of grain in England gets nine loads of manure to one load given to the acre in France.

A further comparison would show that the acknowledged superiority of English cattle, sheep and other domestic animals, over those of France, or any other country for that matter, is due more to the superiority in quality and quantity of the meadows and pastures of that wonderful island than to anything else. If we turn our attention to other countries we shall find that the amount and character of grasses grown may always be taken as a measure of the degree of advancement to which their agriculture has reached. It must be borne in mind that this statement holds good only of the cultivated grasses, but of these it is perhaps universally true.

Under this test the agricultural system of Tennessee falls very low. It is a notable fact, often observed and commented upon,

that the great leading, dominating error in the farming of Tennes-
ee has been, and is, the putting too much land in corn and oats,
and too little in grass. Under this system a very large breadth of
the land has been well-nigh ruined. Indeed, the damage is so
serious that some change has come to be absolutely necessary.
Judging from the experience of other countries, the one and only
thing capable of redeeming this almost ruined land and saving the
farmers from absolute bankruptcy, is grass.

Fortunately, the climate, soil and geographical locality of Tennessee all combine to render it by nature a grass region. In all the
essentials to success in this great branch of agriculture, but few sections of the United States surpass East and Middle Tennessee,
while the northern part of West Tennessee is well suited to many
grasses. It is not unreasonable to anticipate at no distant day,
under an improved system of farming, these natural capabilities
will be thoroughly and judiciously developed, and where now are
only vast wastes and forest wilds, trackless and uncultivated, rich
pastures will bloom and countless cattle roam. But no such result
can come without a radical change in the system of farming.

From the circumstance of the peculiar position of Tennessee as
a border State to the cotton belt, she has lost much time in agricultural progress. The large returns of the cotton planters South,
and the wonderful ease with which they achieved great wealth, induced those living near to attempt the same role that succeeded so
well further south.

Tennessee posesses in her bosom all the elements of a grazing
country. Scarcely a foot of land exists in all her borders that will
not in an eminent degree meet the wants of some one or other of
the grasses. Living streams of water, fed by perennial springs, as
sweet as those of Castalia, hasten down the mountain slopes and
lazily meander through the beautiful valleys. Being midway between the lakes and the gulf, we live just where the warm, moist
southern winds encounter the condensing blasts of the north, so
that we are rarely the sufferers from droughts. In fact, nature intended this State as a grazing region, while man in his thirst for
riches has made it what it is.

Grass is wealth. As lowly and humble as it appears, it comprises
about one-sixth of all the vegetation of the world. It nourishes

more animals than all other food combined, and furnishes all the elements for the growth of animals.

Grasses are divided into two general classes, natural and artificial. the former includes those grasses with long, simple, narrow leaves, with a prominent mid-rib or vein in the center, and smaller ones running parallel to it, and at the base the leaf divides and clasps the stem in such a way that the stem seems to pass through it. As a rule the stem is hollow and closed at the joints, though a few are solid stemmed. The classification of grasses would be impossible were their general appearance only considered. So great are the changes produced by modes of culture, by soil and climate, botanists, to arrive at the precise plant, therefore, have adopted characteristics that undergo no change, such as flowers, etc. From the rule of botanists in giving all plants technical names, it would be a difficult matter to recognize an old familiar friend under the new guise of a generic term; but we will endeavor, by giving also the name in common use, to remove this difficulty and bring them within the comprehension of any one who will take pains to properly read the descriptions.

Artificial grass includes all leguminous plants, such as clover, peas, beans, etc., while cereals, such as maize, wheat, oats, barley, rye, rice, sorghum, dhouro, chocolate-corn and broom-corn, though really true grasses, are generally classed with the artificials.

To one not acquainted with the subject, the facility with which grass scatters and diffuses itself is very surprising. But it seems that so important a vegetation should not be subject to the fancies or caprices of man. The seeds are prepared in such a way, that they are self-sowers. It is this remarkable facility of transportation that has given rise to the surmise of many, that it grows by spontaneous generation. Some of the seeds have hooks, and by these they fasten to any passing animal and are carried for miles. Others lie undigested in the crops of birds, or maws of animals, and are scattered with the dejectæ. Snows gather them on the hill-sides and bear them far away on the melting torrents, and scatter them, mayhap, along some foreign shore. The air also assists in this, and lifts them on its wings and they fly in all directions. When grass once stands, even if a passing beast cuts off its annual supply of seed, its rhizomes or creeping roots thrust their tender spongioles through the yielding soil, and thus many a field is clothed with verdure. And besides, many of the grasses are perennials, and though torn and tramped by stock, they gather new strength for another year, and push on their foothold.

There is a large class resembling the grasses in general appearance, but very different in the physical structure and nutritive elements. I allude to the rushes and sedges, of which there are over five hundred varieties growing in the United States, and eighty of them are found in Tennessee. What is commonly known as "broomsedge" is not a sedge at all, but a true grass, while the well-known "seed-tick" grass is a sedge.

There is a simple method of separating the grasses from these rushes and sedges, which will be briefly stated.

The sheath of sedges is a hollow tube, through which the stems pass, and it cannot be removed without tearing it open. This is not the case with grass, as the sheath can be stripped down, it being open to the joint. Besides, the leaves of all grasses are two-ranked, that is, the stem has leaves on each side, some opposite, others alternate, but always only on two sides. The leaves of sedges are three-ranked, or come out on three sides of the circle of a stem. In other words, the stem forms a circle of 360 degrees. The grass leaves are 180 degrees from each other, and the sedge leaves are 120 degrees apart.

In the grass-like rush the flowers are divided into six points, within which are six stamens and a triangular ovary containing three seeds. A grass has never but one seed to the ovary.

The English farmer is able to take long leases of farms from the rich landholder, at from $20 to $50 per annum rent. How does he pay this extravagant rent and support his family? He could not do it in any other manner than by improving, manuring and increasing the meadows with which they are constantly set. A Tennessean will manure his garden, and sometimes his corn land; but whoever thinks of spreading manure on his meadows? Yet the Englishman will spend large sums of money, and devote labor through the whole winter, in accumulating a large compost heap to apply to his meadows! The result may be imagined. While the Tennessee meadows will average from 800 to 1,500 pounds of hay to the acre; English meadows will make from two to five tons on land that has no other advantage than the care bestowed on it by the owner.

Besides this, the grass grown in a damp, cold climate is never so sweet and nutritious as that raised under a warm sun and with a quick growth. In this State there is an occasional drought that begins in June or July, interfering seriously with the development of the later crops. But such a condition of climate is scarcely known in the earlier months during the growth of the grass crops. Yet there is with the spring rains a degree of temperature unknown to the Englishman, a degree sufficiently high to give grass all the necessary heat to enable it to attain its full supply of sugar and nitrogen from the soil.

The beautiful lands of Kentucky and Missouri, to say nothing of the Northern States, still retain a great value, and are in demand at high prices. It is because these States have more land in meadows, while broad stretches of valuable pastures and prairies dot the landscape in every direction. Poor land will not make much grass, and without a great outlay of capital, land cannot be placed in first-class order at once. But it only requires a start, and then the persevering, provident farmer will soon see his farm blossoming as the rose. Land in Europe not infrequently reaches the sum of $1,000 per acre for purely agricultural purposes, while here it is a difficult matter to extract, with our best farming, $50 per acre, and then the expenses are to be drawn from that meagre sum.

Let us draw a comparision between our leading staples. Cotton here will make on average land 800 pounds seed cotton per acre. This at the usual price makes $20 per acre. Corn will produce on good land eight barrels per acre, and at $2.00, the laborer will get $16. Tobacco, our most remunerative crop, on good land will make 800 pounds of leaf, which is about $50 to $60 per acre. Wheat will make, on good land, fifteen bushels per acre, and at $1 will yield about $15. Taking the cost of production from these amounts, the average farmer will not have left, at the best, more than twelve dollars per acre. A good meadow, in full bearing, with ordinary care, will yield, with two cuttings, at least two tons per acre. The cost is altogether in harvesting, while the trouble of sending to market is no greater than either of the other crops. This, at the price for which it has been selling for several years, will be $20 per ton. Here, then, is a difference in actual receipts of almost double that obtained from other crops, nothing paid out for production, and besides the land can be enriched year by year, until it attains an almost fabulous fertility; nor is this all. The amount of hay produced from a single acre can be increased almost to any extent by the application of stimulating manures. If then, land in Europe can produce five tons of hay per acre, and sell for $1,000 per acre, why cannot Tennessee lands, far better naturally, and in a more genial climate, be made to rival these results? One thing only prevents, and that is the fatal apathy and want of enterprise on the part of the land owners. It is the thirst for immediate returns. To create this state of tillage, it will be necessary to proceed slowly, and look for no returns of consequence for one or two years. Pressing necessities weigh upon the farmer, and he thoughtlessly drives on in the same interminable furrow, regardless of the loss of time and fertility. The Northern husbandman bales his hay, and is able to ship it to all parts of the South in search of a market, and after paying heavy railroad charges, is still able to sell his produce at a remunerative price. The Southern man has no freight charges to tax his hay, and yet he is content to let his Northern rival enjoy, without competition, this great market. When will our eyes be opened to our interests, is a question often asked, but difficult to answer.

A capitalist invests his money in United States bonds, and without risk or labor contentedly cuts off his coupons and enjoys his ease, while the merchant, with the same capital, is harrassed to death meeting bills, collecting accounts, and watching with unceasing vigilance the turn of the markets. So it is with farmers. A prudent farmer will invest his farm capital in grass, and he contentedly watches the growth of the grass and the browsing of his cattle, while his neighbor raising corn and cotton, is busy all the year in cultivating his crops, watching his laborers, buying mules, bacon and hay from his more prudent friend, and when he counts his receipts at the end of the struggle, he will find his neighbor has absorbed the greater part of them. Not only this, but a stranger appears in the country desirous of investing in land, and while he would turn from the cotton plantation at ten or twelve dollars per acre, he would gladly invest in the grass farm at forty or fifty dollars per acre.

Land that will yield ten or fifteen dollars per acre clear of the expense of cultivation, cannot be supposed, and is not entitled to the same value with land that will produce thirty or forty dollars on the same breadth. And yet the farmers of Tennessee hesitate to pursue this course. Gulliver, in the midst of his extravaganzas, uttered a truism that will go down to all ages, when he said " the man who makes two blades of grass grow where one grew before, is a great public benefactor ; " and when the citizens of Tennessee look at their own interest in a proper light, they will realize this truth, and then by acting upon it, double or even quadruple the intrinsic value of the lands of the State.

Grass means less labor, less worry, fewer hands, more enjoyment, finer stock and more charming homes, and as a consequence, happier families, more education, more taste and refinement, and a higher elevation of the moral character. Let grasses be sown and our homes beautified, and there will be more contentment, more satisfaction, less gloom and despondency, less carping and discontent.

MEADOW GRASSES.

The following are the most trustworthy grasses for the meadow in the latitude of Tennessee. I give both the common and scientific names, the average number of pounds in a bushel, the number of seed in an ounce, and depth of soil at which the greatest number of seeds will germinate:

Common Names.	Scientific Names.	No. lbs. in bushel.	No. Seeds in oz.	Depth soil in inches at which the greatest number of seeds will germinate.
Timothy	Phleum pratense	44	74000	½ inch.
Herd's-grass or Red Top	Agrostis vulgaris	12	425000	¼ inch.
Orchard Grass	Dactylis glomerata	12	40000	½ inch.
English Rye Grass	Lolium perenne	18 to 30	15000	¼ to ½ in.
Italian Rye Grass	Lolium Italicum	15	27000	0 to ½ in.
Millet	Panicum miliaceum			
Gama Grass	Tripsacum dactyloides			
Meadow Oat Grass	Avena pratense	5½	118000	0 to ¼ in.
Means Grass	Sorghum halapense			
Red Clover	Trifolium pratense	64	16000	0 to ½ in.
Alsike Clover	Trifolium hybridum	64	16000	0 to ½ in.
Sapling Red Clover	Trifolium erectum	64	16000	0 to ⅞ in.
Crimson Clover	Trifolium incarnatum	64	16000	0 to ½ in.
Lucerne	Medicago sativa	60	12000	
Sainfoine or Esparsette	Onobrychis sativa	26	10280	½ to 1 in.

TIMOTHY—(*Phleum pratense.*)

This grass is known in New England as Herd's grass, from a Mr. Herd, who found it growing wild in New Hampshire, and introduced it into cultivation. Further south, however, this name is only applied to Red Top, or *Agrostis vulgaris.*

Mr. Timothy Hanson carried it from New York to Carolina, and from him it is known as timothy grass.

Its leaves are abundant near the ground, but those on the stalk are comparatively few. Like most other meadow grasses, it attains its greatest value as a food before the seeds are ripe. The latter are very abundant and highly nutritious. From ten to thirty bushels are made on good land.

It ripens late, and consequently favors the farmer very much, as he is able to save his wheat before cutting and curing his hay. It was a common custom at one time to sow it with clover, as it added to the value of the hay, and from the strength of its tall stems it prevented the clover from lodging, but the fact of ripening so much later than clover, causing a great loss from shrinkage, has done away with this practice, especially as orchard grass is so much superior in that respect. Timothy is not suitable for pasturing, having scarcely any aftermath. Besides, the roots are easily destroyed if the stems are taken off below the first joint, this much being required for their vitality. For this reason, also, it is necessary to be careful to *set the blade of the mower sufficiently high to leave the first joint intact.* The roots of this grass are both fibrous and bulbous. Its bulbs have but few rootlets starting out from them, the plant depending for its support principally on the store of nourishment laid up within the bulbs. If, therefore, the stem is shaved off entirely, the bulbs, being deprived of all nourishment, throw out tubers all around, and these send up shoots, seeking food in the air, but they are feeble, and, if spared by the frosts of winter, are so crippled they fall an easy prey to the scorching suns of summer. For the same reason pasturing will effectually destroy a timothy meadow, if persisted in. The stock will bite off all foliage, leaving the roots to perish, or if hogs are allowed to run on it, they quickly discover and destroy the succulent bulbs. When about half the blossoms turn brown, and at least the upper part of the spike or head is still purple, a yellowish spot will make its appearance at or near the first joint, and this is the true indication for the harvest to begin, for this spot will soon extend, if allowed to remain, to the spike, and the whole plant will be a stem of wood. The appearance of this spot also tells of the maturity of the bulbs, and they are not so liable to injury from cutting as before. If this joint is left, the tubers will remain green and fresh during the entire winter; but their destruction is inevitable if it is taken away at any time during the year These remarks do not apply with equal force to timothy when it has a fibrous root, but the two kinds are so intimately mingled there is no practical difference.

Timothy stands at the head of all grasses in its nutritive qualities. A specimen taken from the field, according to the above directions, yielded on analysis: Water, 57.21; flesh-forming principles, 4.86; fat-forming principles, 1.50; heat-producing principles, 22.85; woody fibre, 11.82, and mineral matters, 2.26, in one hundred parts.—(Way.) A comparison of its relative value as a food will be made further on. But the above nutritious specimen will never be produced, if the plant is allowed to stand too long. On the contrary, as a food it would become woody and worthless, all its starch, sugar, albuminoids and other nutritive principles having been deposited in the seeds, and the stalk is nothing more than a woody support.

Cattle fed on this kind, or on hay that has been allowed to get wet and ferment, will quickly lose their flesh and the hair become rough.

Timothy is exhaustive to the soil, and, being a heavy feeder, requires attention. No crop can be raised on ground that will not extract a certain amount of its vitality, but unless something is taken the farmer would receive nothing. Therefore, it is the duty of the farmer to supply by manure the deficiency that occurs; and this is made the more apparent from the fact that the man who applies the most manure will invariably get the best returns for his labor. On good rich land—bottom is best—timothy will make two tons per acre. By a heavy application of compost or manure from the barn-yard, it can be raised to five tons, and the straw lengthened from two feet, its usual height, to five and even six feet, and from the same cause, the heads from two inches to twelve inches in length.

It is a great and sure bearer of seeds, but the seeds are easily destroyed by heat in the mow, unless precautions are used in caring for them.

The time of sowing is various. If sown in the spring it is liable to be killed by summer heat, and if sown late in autumn it runs the same risk with frost. It is, therefore, bad policy to run the risk of not only losing the cost of seed, but also the labor of preparing the ground. Much must be left to the judgment of the farmer in selecting a suitable day, but it is safe to say that it should always be sown in the fall, early enough to get a root strong enough to resist winter killing. If sown in a very dry soil, it will incur the further danger of germinating from dews, and of being killed by the sun. Select the time when the ground is moist, and the days not excessively hot. The quantity of seed per acre is various, but the sower who spares his seed will reap in proportion. Not less than twelve pounds, if mixed, and if alone, at least three gallons of clean seed will be required to secure a good stand. But it will be better to test the seeds beforehand, for a failure from bad seeds will cause a year's delay.

Timothy does best on rich alluvial, moist land; but any rich land, whether upland or lowland, will produce it, if proper attention is given. Wherever calcareous loam exists it can be profitably put to timothy. It will not grow to any extent at a greater elevation than 4,000 feet above the sea, but on any less height there is no grass capable of greater diffusion.

In order to secure a stand of timothy, the following simple rules may be adopted :

1. Be sure of your seed by testing them before sowing.

2. Put plenty of seed on the ground ; if too thin, it will require time to turf over ; if too thick, it will quickly adjust itself.

3. Sow early enough to enable the seed to get a foothold before winter sets in. Late fall and winter sowings are always precarious. September is best, if there is no drought, otherwise wait for a " season."

4. Unlike other grasses, timothy will not admit of pasturage. The nipping of stock will destroy the bulbs.

5. NEVER CUT THE SWARD BELOW THE FIRST JOINT.

6. Be sure to have the ground well pulverized.

It is necessary to impress one idea that has already been stated. Do not allow the timothy to stand longer than the time that the yellow spot appears near the first joint, as it will from that time ripen very rapidly, and be worthless. General Harding, before the Farmers' Club, called attention to the fact, that the greatest enemy of timothy is blue-grass. If stock is allowed to pass from a blue-grass pasture at will, to a meadow of timothy, they will quickly sow the meadow in blue-grass, and the latter will, in a short time supersede the former. In the meeting above alluded to, timothy being the subject of discussion, Gen. Harding being called on for his views, said "he had had considerable experience with timothy. He regarded timothy the most valuable of all the grasses for hay, and more especially for hay that must be handled or shipped or baled. He had tried several varieties. Before the introduction of blue-grass our timothy meadows lasted almost without limit, and produced year after year for twenty or thirty years. But since we have been growing blue-grass more extensively, it gets into our timothy meadows and in a few years will root it out; so now, in buying my timothy seed, I look more carefully for blue-grass seed than for the seed of any noxious weeds. I would rather sow dock —I would rather sow anything in my timothy than blue-grass. Still I value blue-grass in its place as the first of grasses, yet it causes more trouble in our meadows than anything else. Again, our seasons have become dryer, and there is much greater difficulty in getting a stand of timothy than formerly. When I commenced sowing meadows, I had no trouble in getting a stand of timothy, whether I sowed the seed in the fall or in the spring, whether I sowed in the fall with wheat or barley, or in the spring with my oats. For many years I never failed. Now I sow in the fall, and the timothy is frequently winter-killed; I sow in the spring, and it is killed by the long droughts of summer. But these difficulties should not deter us; we should continue to sow, and persevere until we get a stand. Hence if I sow in the fall and my timothy is killed, I sow in the spring; if it is then killed, I sow again and again until I succeed. I have never given up, and have never entirely failed after repeated efforts. I got a good stand of timothy many years ago with a gallon of seed to the acre, now I would recommend not less than one and a half gallons, or even a peck of seed to the acre. Again, the better the stand you get, and the thicker your grass comes up, the more will it keep out the weeds. The white blossom, like the blue-grass, has also increased largely, and seems to be yet increasing. That is a troublesome weed for our meadows, still it is not as pernicious as it seems to the inexperienced. True, you cannot sell white blossom in the market, but if you expect to consume the hay at home, and make your timothy with a large amount of white blossom in it, you will find you will have good hay. Stock will eat it, and readily; mules and cattle seeming to do almost as well upon it as upon the timothy alone.

"I know that some differ from me in considering the white blossom as troublesome as any other plant, and throw it away. I have some hands to run along the windrow and pick out the white blossoms, and make hay of the white blossoms alone. It pays very well for the labor of separating it. I will not throw the white blossom away, for it is valuable. I stack it in my pastures and let the cattle go to it at will during the winter. I also stack my straw, and that helps the cattle.

"Now, what is the proper time to cut timothy? Some would say as soon as it blooms; others would say after it has bloomed and the bloom has fallen. If I could cut it all on the day I thought it would make the best hay, I would cut it just about the time it has lost the largest portion of its bloom. If you cut it too green—like green fodder—the stalk will shrivel and, after being cured, the stalk will break short; but if allowed to get a little riper the stalk will bend.

"How much sun should it have? This is a question that can only be determined by experience. The proper time to put it up is when it has had as little sun as possible, so you are assured it will not mould. If there is too much moisture in it, it will mould, and thereby injure the hay. If the weather is settled, it will cure better in cocks, but all these things must be governed by circumstances."

It is highly propable that the reason Gen. Hardings meadows fail in six or seven years, is the fact, he admits, of pasturing them. It is a well ascertained fact that timothy will not bear pasturing, and attention to this and leaving the first joint uncut will most probably make our meadows again live twenty or thirty years.

At the meeting of the Stock Breeders' Association in February, 1878, Gen. W. H. Jackson said that the best forerunner of timothy is Hungarian grass. If this is sown in the summer and harvested in August or September, and timothy sown upon the stubble and harrowed in, the best stand could be obtained. The Hungarian grass destroys all noxious weeds, and gives a certain degree of compactness to the soil necessary to secure a good stand of timothy.

RED-TOP—HERD'S GRASS—(*Agrostis vulgaris.*)

It was introduced from England, where it was known as Bent grass. When first cultivated it went by the name of English grass. There are many species now raised in England, which are still known as Fine Bent. It is scattered over the whole State, and but few old pastures are free from it, but there it is so dwarfed by close grazing and treading that it shows to but little advantage. It is commonly called in these situations fine-top.

Next in importance to timothy as a meadow grass stands Herd's grass. Unlike the former, it also makes a good grazing grass—in fact, grazing is necessary to its preservation, as, if allowed to go to seed a few years, it dies out. It loves a moist soil, and on swampy places that will grow scarcely anything else, Herd's grass will thrive wonderfully.

It is the most permanent grass we have, and by means of its long, creeping roots, will, even if sown too thin, quickly take possession of the ground. It is greedily eaten while young and tender, in the spring, by all kinds of stock, and affords a fine nourishing-hay, though in less quantity per acre than timothy. It grows from two to three feet high, and with its purplish panicles, when in full bloom, presents a most charming sight in its soft, feathery undulations.

It is oftener mixed with other grasses than sown alone, especially with timothy and clover. But it fails to come into harvest as early as clover, and the same objections may be urged against it that are to timothy. It yields, on moist bottom land, from one and a half to two tons per acre, but on uplands it is not a good producer. On thin lands it will not gain a sufficient height to justify harvesting at all. It withstands the effects of drought much better than timothy. In England it is supposed to grow best on sandy soils. Its effects when fed to milk cows are to greatly enrich and yellow the butter, and European dairymen think they cannot do without it in their pastures. By the Wopurn experiments at the time of flowering, it yielded 10,209 pounds of grass, which lost in drying 5,615 pounds, and furnished 532 pounds of nutritive matter. Cut when the seeds were ripe, it yielded 9,528 pounds of grass, which lost exactly half its weight in drying, and afforded only 251 pounds of nutritious matter. From this it would appear that this grass is doubly as valuable for feeding purposes when cut at the time of flowering.

For stopping gullies in old fields it is superior to blue-grass, as it will throw its long, searching roots from the top down the sloping banks of the washes, and fasten to every patch of good soil at the bottom, and then from every joint starts up a stalk to get a fresh hold. It affords a very good aftermath from which, in wet falls, a fair crop may be cut. Unless well tramped in the late fall it is liable to form tufts that rise out of the soil from the effects of freezing, and is destroyed. Therefore, after cutting, let on the stock, and their feet will insure a good turf, and besides, will destroy weeds. But the cattle should be taken off the pasture after rains have filled the earth with water, or it will become too rough for the proper use of the mower.

The quantity of seed per acre, when sown alone, is about one bushel. The seed is usually sold in the chaff, it being difficult to separate it.

The time for havesting is when it is in full flower, or as soon thereafter as possible, when all the elements that are necessary to form the seeds are still in the stalk and leaves. Left to ripen fully it becomes woody and innutritious.

Many pursue the plan of sowing the timothy and Herd's grass together, as they ripen together, and the Herd's grass being much lower than the former fills in well, and the two will make a more

2

abundant yield than either separate. But one requires pasturage, and that will destroy the other.

It should be sown in September, unless sown on wheat, and then as early as practicable, to enable the roots to get sufficient depth to resist the cold of winter. If sown alone it will, like timothy, make about a half crop the ensuing year, but it is usually sown with grain, wheat, rye or barley. There are a great many marshy spots in Tennessee, especially on the Tennessee and Mississippi rivers, so full of water that nothing can be cultivated on them, and on these fine crops of Herd's grass could be secured every year, which would certainly be far preferable to allowing them to run to waste. These bottoms are usually of surprising fertility, and would go far to supply the great deficiency of hay, and obviate the necessity of importing from our more thrifty Northern neighbors. It is a perennial, and if properly tramped every autumn will keep good an indefinite length of time.

This grass also finds a most congenial soil throughout West Tennessee, in many places in that division of the State attaining the height of five feet. It is probably better adapted to all the soils of the State than any other grass. I have seen it growing in princely luxuriance 6000 feet above the sea on the bald places of the Unaka Mountains. It flourishes upon the slopes and in the valleys of East Tennessee. It yields abundantly upon the sandstone soils of the Cumberland Table-land, and beautifies the rolling surfaces of the Highland Rim. In the Central Basin it sparkles in the beauty of its verdure, and is second only to red clover and timothy as a meadow grass. No other grass is sown so much for hay upon the lands lying at the western base of the Cumberland Table-land. In Warren county especially it is highly esteemed for its longevity and fruitfulnes.

ORCHARD GRASS—(*Dactylis Glomerata.*)

Whether a native of America or Europe, or indigenous to both countries, it is well known that orchard grass is diffused more extensively than any other grass, growing all over Europe, the northwestern parts of Africa, and in Asia Minor. Known as cock's foot in England for many centuries, it was not appreciated as a forage plant until sent to that country from Virginia. It is a perennial, and grows upon congenial soils anywhere between 35 and 47 degrees north latitude. It likes a soil moderately dry, porous, fertile and inclined to be sandy. On stiff clay soils retentive of moisture, the roots do not acquire such a vigor as to give a luxuriant top growth. The feebleness of the roots upon such a soil makes them liable to be thrown up by the earth. It may be grown successfully on a lean, sterile soil, by a top dressing of stable manure, yielding during a moderately wet season from two to three crops. In its rapid growth in early spring lies one of its chief merits, furnishing a rich bite for cattle earlier than almost any other grass. It also grows later in the fall. It is very hardy when well set, makes a great yield, grows rapidly and vigorously upon suitable soils, supplies a rich, nutritious hay, which, compared with timothy, is in value in the proportion of 7 to 10. It starts out early in spring, and comes into blossom about the time of red clover. It attains a height, upon good soils, of three feet, though upon soils of great fertility it sometimes reaches the height of five feet. After being cut, it springs up rapidly, sometimes in rainy weather growing three or four inches within a week. This quality of rapid growth unfits it for a lawn grass unless cut every week.

Nevertheless, this very quality makes it stand unrivalled as a pasture grass. The Hon. John Stanton Gould says in his essay upon this grass: "The laceration produced by the teeth of cattle, instead of injuring, actually stimulates it to throw out additional leaves, yielding the tenderest and sweetest herbage."

The chief objection to orchard grass is that it grows too much in stools or tussocks. This can be remedied by sowing a larger quantity of seed per acre. Never less tban two bushels (14 pounds to the bushel) per acre should be sown, and two and a half bushels would even be preferable. Mr. Gould says that if the meadows are dragged over in spring with a fine toothed harrow, and then rolled, this disposition will be completely overcome. The disposition to stool can also be checked by sowing with other grasses. A half gallon of clover seed, one gallon of Herd's grass, and two bushels of orchard grass, per acre, sown about the 25th of March, in our latitude, will make an excellent pasture. By the middle of June, upon good soils, the amount of forage will equal the best fields of clover. It should not, however, be pastured the first season until August, however tempting it may be. In this many Tennessee farmers have made a mistake. By pasturing before the roots are well established much of the grass is pulled up and destroyed. I have met with many farmers who condemned the orchard grass for want of hardiness and endurance, but in every case the fault was with the farmer himself in pasturing too early.

Orchard grass grows well in the shade, and hence its name. It withstands, hot, dry weather better than any other valuable grass. Three good crops of leafy hay, if the weather is seasonable, may be counted on after the first year, but only one will blossom.

The analysis by Prof Way of the green grass in blossom gives the following result:

	Per cent.
Water.	70.00
Fatty matter	0.94
Flesh formers.	4.06
Heat producers	13.30
Woody fibre	10.11
Ash	1.59

Analysis by Scheven and Ritthausan gives:

Water	65.00
Fat	.80
Flesh formers	3.00
Heat producers	12.60
Woody fibre	16.10
Ash	2.40

The hay made of orchard grass, as analyzed by Wolff and Knop, gives:

Water	14.3
Organic matter	81.1
Ash	4.6
Albuminoids	11.6
Carbohydrates	40.7
Crude fibre	28.9
Fat	2.7

It is of great importance that the seed from hardy plants be sown. In no department of agriculture does the old maxim "like produces like" obtain in a greater degree than in this grass. Seed from weakly, sickly plants will produce the same kind of offspring, however fertile the soil may be. Messrs. Lawson & Son, by selecting the best seed, and sowing for several years none but the best of each generation, established a new variety of orchard grass, known by its great size and vigor as the giant cock's foot. Let farmers be careful, therefore, in saving seed to sow from the most vigorous growth.

The reason why so many bare spots are seen in pastures and meadows of this grass is due to two causes: First—The land is generally not half prepared to receive the seed; and second, there is a penny wise and pound foolish policy in sowing too few seed. Let the land be well broken by deep and thorough plowing, and then be finely pulverized by repeated harrowings. Sow the seed, the thicker the better, and run a light brush or harrow over the land so as to cover the seed slightly. To sum the whole matter up, "plow the land deep, pulverize the soil well, be generous as to the quantity of seed, let that seed be good, sow it evenly, give the land as good treatment afterwards as is given to meadow lands in timothy."

Its chief superiority over timothy lies in the value of its aftermath. It will improve under depasturing when a timothy meadow would be rendered worthless.

To sum up the merits of this grass:

1. It is better suited to every variety of soil than any other.

2. It will grow with greater rapidity than any other grass, and for this reason will sustain a large number of animals, and is excellent for soiling purposes.

3. It will grow in the shade. This quality will enable the farmer to utilize their woodlands as pasture, and so make them a source of profit.

4. It will resist drought better than any other grass. The hot summers make this a very valuable quality in any grass. Often in July and August the pastures become so parched as to afford but a small amount of grazing. Orchard grass then comes to the rescue and supplies the deficiency.

5. It is both a pasture and a hay grass. After a crop of hay has been taken off in June, the aftermath will furnish a good pasture throughout the remainder of the summer.

6. It may be sown in the spring or fall with small grain or alone. It is best not to sow it with grain, as the extra production of grass, when sown alone, is worth more than the grain and grass grown together.

ENGLISH RYE GRASS.—(*Lolium perenne.*)

This was the first grass cultivated in England, and is a great favorite, occupying the same position there that timothy does with us. It is but little cultivated in the United States, though some successful experiments have been made with it in Tennessee. It is of quick growth, and will sometimes yield forty bushels of seed per acre. It produces a nutritious herbage. There are no less than seventy varieties produced in England.

One of the most valuable species of this grass is the *Lolium Italicum* mentioned below.

ITALIAN RYE GRASS.—(*Lolium Italicum.*)

Prof. Way gives the following analysis of this grass: Water, 75.61; flesh-forming principles, 2.45; fatty matters, .80; heat-producing principles, 14.11; woody fibre, 4.82; mineral substances, 2.21.

This grass has been lately introduced from Europe, where it is said to be more universally adapted to all sorts of climates than any other grass, and is very popular there. It grows from two to three feet high, and on moist, rich land, will perhaps bear cutting as frequently as a soiling or green forage crop, as any other grass, affording a succession of green cuttings until late in the fall. It can be forced by manures and irrigation to a greater extent than any other known species of hay.

However, as can be seen from its analysis, it has, when green, nearly half less nutrient properties than timothy, and unless the farmer wishes to cut it as a green food, it has no advantages over the latter. It is an annual with a fibrous root, and bears grazing well. The time of sowing is early fall, and ten pounds of seed are required per acre, a bushel weighing eighteen pounds. It is a valuable grass for Southern farmers, where hay is scarce and high. Being sown in the fall, the farmer will be enabled to cut it early in the spring, thus giving the stock a change from corn alone to succulent hay. It has been fully tested in Georgia, and has given great satisfaction. It gives a fine color to the butter of cows fed on it, and they eat it with great relish. It withstands the hottest suns of summer, as well as the frosts of the severest winter. It must be sown alone, as it will quickly choke and destroy clover or other grasses. Its yield per acre, according to received authority, is immense. Mr. Dickens, of England, sowed it on a stiff, clay soil, well manured, cut it ten times during one year—the first time ten inches in March; April 13th again; May 4th a third time; May 25th a fourth time; June 14th again; July 22d a sixth time, with ripe seed and three loads of hay to the acre. Immediately after each cutting it was manured with liquid manure, the produce of each crop increasing with the temperature of the atmosphere, from three quarters of a load, the first cutting, to three loads the last. He discontinued manuring now, thinking its growth would be terminated in bearing seed, but he afterwards cut four crops from it. On the 26th of January following, it measured sixteen inches in height. The last cutting was October 30th, and on the 8th of April a crop of twenty-two inches high was cut from it. "I was desirous to know the exact amount taken per acre for the year, and it amounted, on a careful measuring and weighing of green hay, to thirteen tons and eighteen hundred and twenty-seven pounds per acre!" (Coleman's European Agriculture.)

It presents a most charming view, with its broad, dark green foliage, and especially in a dry year, when vegetation is parched up all around, it does not show any signs of losing its fresh, living, luxuriant growth. Although an annual, a meadow of this grass may be made perennial by scattering fresh seed over the ground every second year, and scratching it with a harrow with sharp teeth. Its unusual ability to withstand the vicissitudes of heat and cold would make it a desirable grass in any thirsty soil, as well as in moist ones, and might possibly be a valuable addition to the soils of the western portion of our State. At least it is worthy of a trial.

Mr. Gould thinks the valuable qualities of this grass may be summed up as follows:

"Its habit of coming early to maturity.

"Its rapid reproduction after cutting.

"Its wonderful adaptation to all domestic animals, which is shown by the extreme partiality they manifest for it, either alone or when mixed with other grasses; whether when used as green food for soiling, as hay or as pasturage, in which latter state its stems are never allowed to ripen and wither like other grasses.

"Its beneficial influence on the dairy, not only augmenting the flow of milk, but improving the flavor of the cheese and butter.

"Its uncommon hardiness and capacity to withstand the vicissitudes of both wetness and dryness."

CRAB OR CROP GRASS.—(*Panicum Sanguinate.*)

This grass must not be confounded with the *Eleusine Indica*, also called crab grass, from its supposed resemblance to crab.

This species is so familiar to every Southern farmer that it would seem to be superfluous to notice it. But as little as it may appear, it is one of our most valuable indigenous grasses.

Crab grass is an annual, and so full of seed is it that it is never necessary to sow it. It is never cultivated alone, which could be easily done by sowing the seed on a smooth surface about the first of June. When the cultivation of a piece of ground ceases, it at once takes possession, and soon furnishes a fine pasture. It grows not only in the cultivated fields, but in old pastures, yards and woods.

It is a fine pasture grass, although it has but few base leaves, and forms no sward, yet it sends out numerous stems, branching freely at the base. It serves a most useful purpose in stock husbandry. It fills all our cornfields, and many persons pull it out for hay. It makes a sweet food, and horses are exceedingly fond of it, leaving the best hay to eat it. Should it be desired to secure a good crop of it, do not pasture the wheat or oat stubble, except with hogs, until the crab grass gets a good start, then take off the hogs and allow it to get into bloom, and if the land is good, there will be a paying quantity to save. It should be sedulously guarded from rain.

MILLET.—(*Panicum Miliaceum.*)

There are a great many varieties of this important grass, and almost every year adds to the list of them. The preference for any variety is arbitrary, yet there are many advantages belonging to all. But so far as the planter is concerned, one description serves for all, as the mode of culture is the same, and the only difference is in the botanic characteristics.

The first millet cultivated in this State was the kind commonly called Tennessee millet. In a few years the Hungarian grass, or millet, became popular. It does not yield so much hay, but it is eaten with more avidity by stock. The Missouri, which is only a modification of the Tennessee; next became the favorite, and then the German millet came and superseded all others. The manner of its introduction was in this wise :

Two Germans came to Tennessee in 1861. One of them brought a little sack of millet seed, about a quart, which he kept in his trunk during the war. At the close of the war he took it out one day, and handing it to a merchant on Market street asked him to give it to some good farmer for planting. The merchant gave it to Mr. James Allen, of Williamson county, one of the best millet seed planters in the State. The crop was the admiration of the whole country, and he gave a half bushel to Dr. W. M. Clark. He planted the entire amount, and wrote concerning it so that the seed sold for from three and a half to five dollars a bushel. It has taken precedence of all other varieties.

Last year the Department at Washington sent out a new variety, called "pearl millet." It has proved, however, to be a variety that has been planted for many years in the extreme Southern States, and is of but little value unless cut as a green forage. It grows rapidly and is eaten with relish by stock. But if allowed to attain full growth or produce seed, it cannot be eaten, as it becomes woody. It may be cut every six weeks through the season, or when it gets high enough to be reached by a mowing blade.

We will now give its cultivation in general and its use, which embraces every variety as well as one.

At one period, it was deemed sufficient food for any stock, without the aid of anything else. The fodder was hay and the seed was corn. But later investigations have demonstrated the fact, that when hay ripens to seed, its usefulness as a hay measurably ceases. Were stock fed exclusively on seed-heads, with a sufficiency of good hay, they would thrive exceedingly well, or if the millet is cut while in the flower, or even when the seed is in the milky state, and fed to stock in combination with grain, they would do well. But even then, it is much inferior to oats, timothy, or Herd's grass. Its special recommendation is, that it yields a larger proportion of hay than other grasses. It requires a rich, dry soil, and will stand almost any amount of droughts, seeming to dry up during the heat, but when it rains it will start off with renewed life, and do as well as ever. It makes large quantities of seed per acre, the Hungarian yielded 30 bushels; the Missouri 40; the Tennessee 50; and the German from 60 to 80 bushels per acre. The Hungarian millet is a better hay than either of the others, but its yield is much less. The Tennessee millet perhaps yields more hay than either of the other three, but the Missouri has more reputation as a feed for cattle. Should it be wished, however, to sow for a money crop, it will be far preferable to sow the German millet. The Hungarian has a small head, a simple spike, while the others have compound spikes, most notably the German. It is easily raised, at less cost than corn, and makes, on good ground, nearly double as many bushels as the latter per acre. For all kinds of fowls it is unsurpassed, and it is a powerful stimulant to laying eggs.

To sow for hay, prepare the ground in a thorough manner, pulverizing it completely, and when the ground is in a sufficiently moist condition, in June, sow the seed, a bushel to the acre. Never sow if the ground is too dry or too wet. If too dry, the seed near the surface will parch in the rays of the sun, and a stand will fail to appear. If too wet, the usual injury to the land occurs, and the crop "frenches" or turns yellow and dwarfs. After sowing, harrow well and the labor is over. The millet will require seventy or eighty days to mature, unless it is sown in July, when it will require a few days longer.

Two crops of Hungarian grass can easily be raised from the same ground annually. A farmer of Davidson county raised a most excellent crop of Hungarian grass, sown the 1st day of September and cut on the 10th of October. Another, of Williamson county, secured a good crop of German millet, sown on the 13th day of August, and cut on the 12th day of October.

For seed, prepare the ground as above described, and then, with a light bull-tongue or skooter plow, run light parallel rows thirty inches apart, and with a tin cup or oyster can that has three or four holes punched in the bottom with a 4-penny nail, walk rapidly along the furrow, and the seed will sift into it from the cup about right for a stand. Cover very lightly with a cotton coverer, and when the seeds begin to sprout, but before they show the sprouts above ground, run over the field with a harrow, so as to loosen the ground and destroy weeds. Afterwards cultivate with a cultivator and double-shovel, one plowing with each being all that is required. It will be necessary to thin out the Tennessee millet with hoes, leaving a mere thread of stems, as it stools prodigiously; but this will be unnecessary with either of the other three, as they scarcely stool at all.

To save it for seed, it must be cut with reap-hooks, taking just enough of the head to enable the laborer to make it into bundles; or if preferred, it can be broken off at the head, taking only the seed, leaving the stubble to renew the soil. They are, after treading out in a barn or on a clean spot, separated from the chaff with an ordinary wheat fan.

This grass is of great value to the renter who has no opportunity of continuing in possession of the land long enough to set a meadow. A crop of millet is a good forerunner for a meadow, as it destroys all the noxious weeds, and leaves the land in a fine condition for timothy or Herd's grass.

GAMA GRASS—(*Tripsacum dactyloides.*)

This is in some sections called sesame grass. It is the largest and one of the most beautiful grasses we have, growing to the height of seven feet. It is abundant throughout the Mississippi Valley, on moist, slushy places. When young and succulent it is eaten with avidity by stock, and makes from its rapid growth, a good soiling or forage crop, but when it gets large its stem is so woody stock refuse to eat it. Its leaves are very large, equal in size to the leaves of corn, but they are rough and hairy.

The grass may be cut three or four times a year, and though in its native state it grows in swamps, it thrives almost equally well on dry or sandy ridges. It will grow where timothy or Herd's grass will not, and consequently is well suited to a large section of our State. The quantity of hay taken from one acre is simply enormous, and resembles very much corn fodder, and as a hay is fully equal to it, and it can be saved at one-tenth the labor required to save fodder. The roots are strong and large as cane roots, so let it be sown where it will not be desired to remove it. However, close grazing for a few years will destroy it.

It is very nutritious and succulent when cut green. The great mass of roots it has will serve to open, loosen and improve the land upon which it grows. It should never be allowed to shoot up the seed stem when desired for hay.

It is with difficulty the seed can be made to vegetate, and therefore it must be propagated by slips from the roots. Prepare the land well, lay off the furrows with a bull-tongue plow two feet apart, and drop a small piece of root about two feet apart in the furrow, covering with a board. The creeping roots will soon meet, and the ground is quickly turfed with it. It should be planted early in September. Of course, the richer the land, whether upland or bottom, the greater the yield, as the time has never yet come when poor land will make better crops of anything than fertile land. I have seen it growing with great luxuriance in Montgomery county.

MEADOW OAT GRASS—(*Avena pratensis.*)

This is a perennial grass, and is a native of Great Britain. It is one of the few grasses that do best on a dry soil. It grows to a height of only eighteen inches in its native pastures. But here it is quite a different grass, and rises to the height of from five to six feet. It will not grow well on moist soils, but on rich upland or good sandy land it grows with vigor. It deserves a place on every farm, as the hay is excellent, and is greedily eaten by stock, and besides, the yield is extremely large. Another advantage is that the seed will be ripe before the hay turns yellow, so that not only the hay will be saved, but a large amount of seed can be secured; upon a barn floor enough will shatter out to supply the wants of most farmers. Or if the farmer wishes to sell the seed, he can cut off the heads with a cradle and let the mower follow for the hay.

Should the autumn prove a wet one, a second crop can be cut, but if there is not sufficient aftermath to justify cutting do not pasture it, but allow it to grow on as long as it will, and about Christmas it will turn over and the tops turn yellow, all prepared for the hungry stock, and it will continue to sustain them until other grasses take its place. However, should it be desired to use it for hay the succeeding year, the stock should be removed about the middle of February.

It will seed in the fall after being sown in the spring, which is the proper time to sow it. Sow two bushels per acre. The seed is very light and chaffy. It is a tussock grass, and does not spread from the roots, consequently the seed must be depended on for a stand. After the first sowing, there will be no difficulty in obtaining seed, as the yield is large. It affords, both for hay and pasture, perhaps more green food than any grass we have.

SORGHUM—(*Halpense.*)

Egyptian Sugar Cane, as its proper name is, is a daughter of the Nile, where it grows fifteen or twenty feet high. So great is its luxuriance there that it has filled all the upper Nile so that a canoe cannot be driven through it. Great numbers of cattle and wild animals resort to it, and, in fact, it is the chief sustenance of ruminants in that country.

When young it is very tender and sweet, the pith being full of sugary juice. The leaves are as large as corn fodder, and very nutritious. It has a perennial root, and so vigorous that when once planted it is a difficult matter to eradicate it. So care must be taken to plant it where it is not intended to be disturbed. The roots are creeping, and throw out shoots from every joint. It is a fine fertilizer, and sown on a piece of poor washed land, will, in a few years restore it to its pristine fertility. But there is really not much difference where it is sown, for a farmer once getting a good stand, will not want to destroy it. It will bear cutting three or four times a year, and, in fact, it has to be done, for when it matures the seed, the stem and leaves are too course and woody for use.

The ground must be well prepared as in other grasses, and in September, the earlier the better, let it be sown one bushel to the acre.

It can be propagated also by the roots by laying off the rows each way, and dropping a joint of the root two feet apart and covering with a drag.

It gives the earliest pastures we have, preceding blue grass or clover a month. Hogs are fond of the roots, and any amount of rooting in it will not injure it. In fact, it is a *stick tight.* It not only thrives well on bottoms, but it will grow just as well on upland, and though poor upland will make little hay, yet it makes a fine pasture. It disappears in the winter altogether, but the first warm weather brings it up, and it grows with astonishing rapidity. On our lands and in our climate it will grow from five to seven feet high, while in South Carolina it will grow twelve feet high.

For soiling purposes it is not equaled by any grass in our knowledge, as it can be cut every two or three weeks.

Many persons object to it on account of its great tenacity of life, matting the soil in every direction with its cane-like roots, and the rapidity with which it will spread over a field, and the difficulty of eradicating it. But these very objections should be its recommendation to owners of worn-out fields; and if it be desired to destroy it, it is only necessary to pasture it closely one year, and then in the fall turn the roots up with a big plow to the freezes of a winter, renewing the breaking up once or twice during the winter, and then cultivating the next spring. The seeds are quite heavy, and weigh thirty-five pounds to the bushel. Every one who has tried it recommends it to the public. But some allowance must be made for the partiality of friends, and it would be well to give it a trial before engaging in its culture to any extent. There would, however, certainly be no risk in sowing it upon those worn-out hill sides, so many of which form an unsightly scar upon the face of nature in Tennessee—the tokens of the past.

A proximate analysis made by the Department of Agriculture at Washington gives :

	Per cent.
Oil	2.26
Wax	.61
Sugar	7.37
Gum and Dextrine	5.14
Cellulose	25.1
Amylaceous cellulose	25.87
Alkali extract	15.58
Albuminoid	13.18
Ash	4.85

Analysis of the ash of the Johnson grass:

	Per cent.
Potassium	3.68
Potassium oxide	35.72
Sodium	.81
Calcium oxide	12.87
Magnesium oxide	0.73
Sulphuric acid	2.96
Phosphoric acid	10.44
Silicic acid	22.21
Chlorine	4.58

RED CLOVER—*(Trifolium pratense.)*

This valuable forage plant was first introduced into England in 1645, during the stormy times of Charles I., and rapidly met with favor throughout the kingdom. It properly belongs to the leguminous family, which includes a considerable number of other forage plants that are called artificial grasses, to distinguish them from the true or natural grasses called *gramineæ.* The botanic name trifolium comes from two latin words, *tres,* three, and *folium,* a leaf, and in England it is often called trefoil. It may always be known by having three leaves in a bunch, and the flowers in dense, oblong, globular heads.

There is no grass, natural or artificial, that is more useful to the farmer or stock-grower than red clover. It has been styled, with some show of reason, the corner stone of agriculture, and this not only on account of its vigorous vitality, but because it adapts itself to a great variety of soils. It is widely diffused, and abounds in every part of Europe, in North America, and even in Siberia. It furnishes an immense amount of grazing, yields an abundance of nutritious hay, and is a profitable crop, considered with reference to the seed alone. But beyond all these, it acts as a vigorous ameliorator of the soil, increasing more than any other forage plant the amount of available nitrogen, and so becomes an important agent in keeping up the productive capacity of the soil, and increasing the yield of other crops.

SOILS ADAPTED TO ITS GROWTH.

Red clover is a biennial plant, and under judicious tillage may be made a perennial, and is specially adapted to argillaceous soils, but it will grow well upon sandy soils, when a "catch" is secured, by the application of a top-dressing of gypsum or barn-yard manure. I have seen it growing with vigor upon the feldspathic soils of Johnson county, upon the sandstone soils of the Cumberland mountain, and upon the sandy loams of West Tennessee, but it finds a more congenial soil in the clayey lands of the valley of East Tennessee, on the red soils of the Highland Rim, and on the limestone loams of the Central Basin.

The clayey lands of West Tennessee have no superior for the production of clover. It often grows upon these lands from four to five feet in height, and forms a mat, when it falls, of great density and thickness. As much as four tons of clover hay have been taken from a single acre. Probably three fourths of the lands in Tennessee will grow clover remuneratively, and of the soils which will not, a large portion is included in the old gullied fields that constitute the shame and mark the thriftlessness of too many of the farmers. It may be set down as an infallible rule in the State of Tennessee that good farming and abundant clovering go together.

SOWING CLOVER.

Clover may be sown in the latitude of Tennessee upon wheat, rye, or oat fields, or alone. Instances have been reported to me where a splendid stand was obtained by sowing after cultivators in the last working of corn in July. This is unusual, however. So is fall sowing. The best time to sow is from the first of January until the first of April. If sown in January or February, the seed ought to be sown upon snow. This is not only convenient in enabling one to distribute the seed evenly over the land, but the gradual melting of the snow, and the slight freezes, bury the seed just deep enough to ensure rapid germination when the warm days of March come on. For the same reason, if sown in March, the seed ought to be sown when the ground is slightly crusted by a freeze. If the sowing is deferred until too late for frosty nights, the land should be well harrowed and the seed sown immediately after the harrow. It will hasten germination and cause a larger proportion of seed to grow, to harrow the land after the seed is sown. With oats, the seeds should be sown after the last harrowing or brushing, with a slight after-brushing to cover them.

A better stand of clover, with less seed, may always be secured by sowing upon land prepared for clover alone. I have often obtained an excellent catch upon " galled " places by breaking the land well, and sowing the seed without any previous or after harrowing.

3

Upon good, fresh, rich soils, where clover has not previously grown, one bushel for eight acres will be sufficient. If the soil is thin and unproductive, one bushel for six acres ought to be sown. If the land has been regularly rotated with clover, one-half the quantity of seed mentioned above will suffice, sometimes much less.

The frequent failure to secure a good stand of clover admonishes the farmers of the State to exercise more care in the seeding. When sown late in the spring many of the seeds sprout, and are killed by dry weather. It would be all the better if the clover seed could be buried a half-inch (or even an inch on loose soils) beneath the surface after the middle of March.

GROWTH AND MANURE.

Red clover rarely makes much growth the first season if sown with grain. Should the weather be very seasonable after harvest, and the land fertile, it will sometimes attain the height of thirty inches and put out blooms, making an excellent fall pasture. When sown alone it will always blossom in August.

As soon as it begins to grow, in early spring, an application of two bushels of gypsum or land plaster, upon granitic or sandy soils, is absolutely necessary to get a good growth.

Baron Liebig, after numerous experiments made with gypsum upon clover, comes to the conclusion that the action of gypsum is very complex; that it indeed promotes the distribution of both magnesia and potash in the soil. He thinks that gypsum exercises a chemical action upon the soil, which extends to any depth, and that in consequence of the chemical and mechanical modification of the earth, particles of certain nutritive elements become accessible to and available for the clover plant, which were not so before.

Though having my mind constantly directed to this point, I have rarely found an application of gypsum beneficial upon clayey loams, but its effects are very apparent on strong limestone soils, such as are found in the Central Basin. Red clover has two growing seasons. It makes its most vigorous growth from the 1st of April until the 15th of June, beginning to bloom usually in the central parts of the State about the 15th of May, and attaining its full inflorescence about the 1st of June. After this, unless depastured by stock or cut for hay, the heads begin to dry up, and stems and leaves begin to fall, forming a mat upon the land. Sometimes this mat is so thick as to catch and concentrate the heats of summer to such a degree as to scald the roots and destroy the clover. Usually it is best after clover has attained its full bloom, either to cut it for hay, or pasture with stock until about the first of July. When the stock is removed, or the clover hay cured and taken off, and there is rain enough, a second crop will spring up from the roots. This second crop is the most valuable for seed, the seed maturing about the last of August, and sooner, if there be copious rains. To make the most abundant yield of clover for grazing, it should be allowed to grow all it will, but never let it make seed, always grazing it down when in full bloom. When grazed down, take off the stock until it blooms again. Several successive crops may thus be made during the summer. The crop of August is unfit for grazing, the large quantity of seed having the effect of salivating stock to such a degree as to cause them to lose flesh.

It is a fact, well attested by English writers, and by observant farmers of this country, that when clover has been frequently sown upon the same land, it not only fails to produce a heavy crop, but fails to appear at all. The land is then said to be " clover sick." The remedy for this is by extending the number of crops in the scale of rotation, so that clover will not come so often upon the same land. By Liebig, clover-sick land is supposed to be caused by the roots of clover impoverishing the subsoil.

Clover has no superior as a grazing plant. When in full vigor and bloom, it will carry more cattle and sheep per acre than blue-grass, Herd's grass, or orchard grass. After it has been grazed to the earth, a few showery days with warm suns will cause it to spring up into renewed vitality, ready again to furnish its succulent herbage to domestic animals. Though very nutritious and highly relished by cattle, it often produces a dangerous swelling called hoven, from which many cows die. When first turned upon clover, cattle should only be allowed to graze for an hour or two, and then be driven off for the remainder of the day, gradually increasing the time of grazing, until they become less voracious in their appetites, never permitting them to run upon clover when wet. Clover made wet by a rain at midday is more likely to produce hoven than when wet by dew. This is because when wet by rain at midday, or after the stalks and leaves are heated by the sun, when taken into the stomach of a cow, this heat generates fermentation much sooner than when the herbage is cool, though wet with the morning dew.

Cattle are more easily affected by clover than horses, because being ruminants, they take in the clover rapidly, filling the stomach at once, without chewing. Digestion is for the time checked, and a rapid fermentation sets in. The remedy found most effective for hoven is to stick a sharp pointed knife about six inches in front of the hip, to the left side of the backbone, and far enough from it to miss the spinal protuberances, and in the thinnest part of the flank. A cow should never be run when affected with hoven, as this treatment only intensifies the pain without affording relief.

Stock should never be turned upon clover until it blooms. The practice of many of our farmers, to turn all the stock upon a clover field early in April, is very destructive. The crown of the clover is eaten out, causing it to perish. The tread of heavy cattle has the same effect.

As a soiling crop red clover is excelled by no crop grown within the State. The practice of soiling in thickly settled communities is one much commended by agricultural writers. An half-acre of clover will supply one cow throughout the months of June, July and August, if cut off and fed in a stall, while twice the amount in pasture, according to some English experimenters, will barely subsist a cow during the same period, and this will depend, of course, upon the luxuriance of the growth. Soiling (that is cutting the grass and feeding it green) is a very desirable practice, near small towns, where many persons own small lots, and desire to keep a milch cow. No other grass, perhaps, will produce a larger flow of milk.

NUTRITIVE VALUE AND CONSTITUENT ELEMENTS OF CLOVER.

The nutritive value of clover was long known by feeders before chemical research demonstrated the same fact. It contains, when cut in bloom, nearly four per cent more nitrogenous food than timothy, and four and a half per cent more than blue-grass. According to Professors Wolff and Knop, in its green state it contains 800 parts in 1,000 of water, about 100 parts more than timothy, and 37 parts in 1,000 of albuminoids or flesh formers. When made into hay, cut when in bloom, and well cured, red clover contains 134 parts in 1,000 of albuminoids, but cut when fully ripe only 94 parts. The albuminoids contain about 16 per cent of nitrogen. Timothy hay has 9.7 per cent of flesh-forming matter, and therefore contains less nitrogen, in the proportion of 15 to 21, than clover hay. Barley has 10 per cent of albuminoids, Indian corn 10.7, rye 11, oats 12, clover 13.4 per cent, so that it appears clover hay will furnish more muscle-producing or nitrogenous food than either corn, rye, oats, or timothy, which gives strength to the statements of many practical farmers, that a crop can be made by feeding clover hay alone to the working animals, and they will keep up under it.

Professor Way gives the following analysis of the red clover when green:

	Per cent.
Water	81.
Albuminoids	4.27
Fatty matter	.69
Heat producing	8.45
Woody fibre	3.76
Ash	1.82

One hundred pounds dried at 212 F. gives the following:

	Per cent.
Albuminoids or flesh-formers	22.55
Fatty matter	3.67
Heat-producers (starch, sugar, gum, etc.)	44.47
Woody fibre	19.75
Ash	9.56

The proportion of fat in the various vegetable products is given in the following table, taken from Prof. S. W. Johnson's " How Crops Grow":

	Fat.
Meadow grass	0.8 per cent
Red clover (green)	0.7 per cent
Meadow hay	3.0 per cent
Clover hay	3.2 per cent
Wheat straw	1.5 per cent
Oat straw	2.0 per cent
Wheat bran	1.5 per cent
Potato, Irish	0.3 per cent
Turnip	0.1 per cent
Wheat kernel	1.6 per cent
Oat kernel	1.6 per cent
Indian corn	7.0 per cent
Pea	3.0 per cent
Cotton seed	34.0 per cent
Flax seed	34.0 per cent

446366

It appears from this table that clover hay has not quite one-half the fat of Indian corn, but having more albuminoids it has nearly three per cent more nitrogenous food. Both should be fed together, the clover to give muscle and the corn to give fat. It also appears that the clover hay is richer in fat than meadow hay.

EFFECTS OF CLOVER UPON SOILS—MANURE FOR.

Numerous facts have taught the farmers of every country where agriculture has flourished, that in many cases the value of the after crop depends upon the preceding crop. In other words, a proper rotation is necessary antecedent to successful farming. The cultivation of some crop with extensive root ramifications will prepare the soil for the subsequent growth of a cereal. But the farmer should not deceive himself. Every crop takes away a part of the available plant-food, and the field has not increased in fertility, but the plant-food has been made more rigidly effective for the production of a crop. "The physical and chemical condition of the fields has been improved, but the chemical store has been reduced." "All plants," says Liebig, "without exception, exhaust the soil, each of them in its own way, of the conditions for their reproduction."

A field, then, which produces more kindly after rotation, is not necessarily more fertile, but is in better *physical condition*. It has already been mentioned, that the mechanical effects of clover upon soils is not the least among its valuable properties. The reaction rendered possible by the penetration into the soil of the long tap-roots, and the effect of the dense shade upon the land have a tendency to increase the productiveness, but may not add to the fertility of the soil.

Guano is found on clayey soils, to largely increase the growth of clover. When used on a wheat field seeded to clover in early spring, a "catch" of clover will be secured on the thinnest spots, and grow luxuriantly. The greatest benefits from an application of guano upon wheat are often obtained in this way. A good stand of clover, however secured, is the best possible preparation of land for a succeeding crop of wheat. And this arises, not only from the available nitrogen which a clover crop supplies, but from the deep and thorough subsoiling which is effected by the deep, penetrating tap-roots of the clover. They often descend to the depth of four feet in search of food, while its broad leaves "absorb carbon from the atmosphere, changing it into solid matter, causing elements in the soil to assume organic forms, rendering them more available as food for other crops." If the soil be robbed of its fertility, the deficient elements must be added before clover will "take."

The best method of pasturing is to wait until about the last of May, when the clover is in bloom, then turn on stock and pasture during the months of June and July, alternating every two weeks with other clover fields, if possible, and turning off the stock the first of August, and allowing the second crop to come forward for seed.

SAVING CLOVER HAY.

The precise period of mowing clover for hay is a question about which there has been much discussion. All will agree that it should be mowed at the time when the nutritive elements—those elements which give strength and produce flesh—are at their maximum. Those who are in the habit of feeding stock find that clover cut about the time of full bloom, when a few of the seeds begin to dry up, and just as the reproductive functions are being brought into play for the maturing of seed, will, pound for pound, produce more fat and muscle than that cut at any other time. The only art in curing hay is to retain as many of the life-giving constituents in it as possible, or to preserve it as near as practicable in the same condition in which it is cut, with the water only abstracted.

The plan generally adopted is to mow the clover in the morning and let it lie in the sun several hours until a wisp, taken up and twisted, will show no exudation of moisture. It is then thrown up into small cocks, say four feet in diameter and four feet high. In these, unless there is appearance of rain, it is allowed to remain for a day or two, when it may be hauled to the barn and stored away without danger of damage. Care should be taken not to let the dew fall upon it as it lies scattered by the mower. The dew of one single night will blacken the leaves and destroy the aroma for which good clover hay is so much prized.

Another plan practiced is to mow it and let it lie just long enough in the sun to wilt, and then wagon it to an open house and lay it upon beams or tier-poles, where it can receive the free action of the air. After a few days it may be packed down without any danger of fermenting. Cured in this way, in the shade, it retains its green color, is fragrant, and makes a most excellent feed. The only objection to this plan is the great amount of room under cover required for curing, and the additional burthen of hauling while green.

Another plan is to haul it up as soon as it wilts, using about half a bushel of salt to the cured ton of hay. A layer a foot or more in thickness may be laid down, over which salt is scattered pretty freely, then another layer and salt, continuing to repeat the operation until the space set apart for hay is filled. A rapid fermentation will ensue, and the hay will be cured by the heat of this fermentation, the salt acting as a preventive against putrefaction. Instead of salt, layers of wheat straw can be substituted. By using straw the clover may be put up in the field. The quantity of straw to be used in the rick or stack depends upon the moisture in the clover—the greener the clover the thicker should be the straw. The straw will act as an absorbent, and during the process will itself be greatly increased in value as food for stock, having imparted to it the flavor and aroma of the clover plant. All the wheat straw on a farm could be utilized in this way, and the amount of manure in the farmer's barn largely increased.

Still another method of curing clover hay is the one practiced in Ireland. The Irish Farmer's Journal, in giving an account of this process of curing clover hay, says:

"The clover intended for hay is mown and left to lie in the swath until 4 o'clock in the afternoon of the following day to dry. Of course these swaths are twelve or eighteen inches thick. They are then raked together in small shocks, which are afterwards made into larger ones, such as would require six or eight horses to draw. Two or more men are kept upon the large ones tramping them down, so as to make them more compact and induce a more speedy fermentation. If the weather is warm, fermentation will begin in a few hours, as will be known by the honey-like smell. When a proper fermentation has begun, the cocks, on being opened, will appear brownish and may be spread. After drying, it may be carried to the hay loft without any danger of a second fermentation."

It should always be borne in mind that clover hay will not shed rain. When stacked out in the field, it should either be thatched or have a thick top--covering of wheat straw or other hay. The

The tedder is thought by many to be indispensable in saving good clover hay. Unquestionably it is of great service, and the hay made by the use of the tedder in dry, hot weather is superior to that made without; but good hay can be and is made by many farmers who never saw a tedder. Clover hay is more difficult to cure than hay from any of the real grasses, and this arises from the fact that it contains more water than other grasses in the proportion of eight to seven. For this reason, also, it is more difficult to keep, being more liable to heat in the mow. It will not bear handling or transportation, and while it will always be a favorite hay for home consumption, it will never be valuable for market purposes. For horses good grass hay is probably better than clover, because it it more digestible, and is not so liable to produce colic. On the other hand, clover is a superior hay for cattle, producing in milk cows a fine flow of milk.

The following table, compiled from analyses made by Wolff, Knop and Way, will exhibit the comparative value of clover and grass hays:

SUBSTANCE.	Water.	Organic matter.	Ash.	Albuminoids.	Carbohydrates.	Crude fibre.	Fat, etc.
Red clover, in bloom	16.7	77.1	6.2	13.4	29 9	35 8	3.2
Red clever, ripe	16.7	77.7	5.6	9.4	20.3	48.0	2.0
White clover	16.7	74.8	8.5	14 9	34 3	25 6	3.5
Alsike clover, in bloom	16.7	75.0	8.3	15.3	39 2	30.5	3.3
Alsike clover, ripe	16.7	78.3	5.0	10.2	23.1	45.0	2.5
Orchard grass	14.3	81.1	4.6	11.6	40.7	28.9	2.7
Timothy	14.3	81.2	4.5	9.7	48.8	32 7	3.0
Kentucky blue grass	14.3	80.6	5.1	8.9	39.1	32.6	3.1

SAVING CLOVER SEED.

It has often been a matter of surprise that Tennessee farmers have not more generally saved their clover seed. The amount of money yearly paid out, for an article which is now considered a prime necessity to good farming, is erroneous. Were the lands of Tennessee incapable of producing clover seed, there would be reason for this expenditure. In point of fact, however, no section of the Union will produce, acre for acre, a larger quantity of clover seed.

Three bushels per acre have often been gathered, although the usual average is about one and a half bushels.

As the first crop of clover, coming to maturity in June, will not perfect its seed, it is necessary to take off the first crop, either by feeding or by mowing for hay, and rely for the seed upon the after crop. The quantity of seed of this crop will depend much upon the weather. Should there be much rain or heavy winds, the yield of seed will be small, but when the weather has been fine and calm, and the seed free from dock or other noxious seeds, the crop will be found as remunerative as any other grown by the farmer. A bushel of clover seed will weigh usually about sixty-four pounds, though sixty pounds is the standard bushel in market.

The seed crop of clover should be allowed to stand until the husks have become quite brown and the seeds have passed the milky state. It should then be mowed and permitted to lie upon the ground until it is well cured. After it is cured rake it up into swaths. Rain will rather benefit than injure it, making it easier to separate the heads from the haulm, which is done by passing through an ordinary wheat separator. A clover huller attachment is adjusted to the separator below the vibrator, which hulls the seeds, and they are separated from the chaff by the fan, care being taken to shut off as much air as possible by closing the sliding doors.

The crop of seed can be largely increased by mowing or feeding off the first crop of clover about the first of June, and then top-dressing with stable manure. The earlier the first crop is cut the larger will be the crop of seed. By treating the clover fields in this way, as much as three bushels of seed have been obtained from an acre. Uplands will yield more seed than bottom lands, but they should be enriched by a liberal application of manure. About the first of September is the time to mow for seed, and the straw will thresh all the better for being exposed to the weather for three weeks. The threshing is usually done in the field, though the haulm may be hauled up after being thoroughly dry, and stacked with a good straw covering, or else stored away under shelter on a good tight floor until it suits the convenience of the farmer to thresh. Care should be taken not to run over or tramp upon the clover after it is dried, as many seeds are thus shelled out and lost. The better plan is to haul to the thresher just as soon as the straw

is in a proper condition to thresh. This will save the trouble and
expense of stacking.

Some farmers prefer to sow in the chaff, believing that a better
stand of clover is thus secured. Usually about thirty bushels in
the chaff are considered equivalent to one of cleaned seed. Of
course this will depend greatly upon the yield of seed, and experiments ought to be made to determine the relative amount to sow
when in chaff.

CLOVER AS A PREPARATORY CROP FOR WHEAT.

No question at the present day pertaining to agriculture is more
deeply interesting to the farmers of Tennessee than how to increase
the yield of the wheat crop per acre, for upon this depends the
profits of this standard crop, one probably more generally grown in
the State than any other. It has also been noted that a soil well
suited to clover is generally well adapted to wheat, but not until the
painstaking investigations of Dr. Voelcker, of England, was the
fact established that the clover plant, by increasing the amount of
available nitrogen in the surface soil, is the very best forerunner
for wheat, unlocking, as it were, the elements in the soil necessary
to a full and perfect development of the wheat crop.

Prof. Way has established the fact that the carbonate of ammonia of rain-water and of manures are so absorbed and so firmly
fixed by the soil that no free ammonia can be present in it.
Neither pure nor carbonic acid water can extract this fixed ammonia from the soil. It must be extracted by the roots of plants. A
plant, therefore, with extensive root ramifications, such as clover,
will extract a much larger quantity than those plants with feebler
roots. The clover roots bring this ammonia or nitrogen to the surface, and on their decay these nitrogenous matters are converted
into nitrates in which the wheat plant finds a most congenial food.
In addition to this, the leaves formed by clover contain a large
amount of nitrogenous matter, and these are dropped upon the surface, increasing the amount of nitrogen available for wheat or other
crops.

ALSIKE CLOVER—(*Trifolium hybridum.*)

This species of clover was introduced into England from Sweden, hence it is sometimes called Swedish clover. It gets the name Alsike from the parish of Alsike, in the province of Upland. It is a perennial found wild throughout many parts of Sweden, Norway and Finland.

Alsike clover, as compared with common red clover, has a slenderer stalk, narrower leaf, and paler colored flowers and foliage. The flower stalks are longer, and the blossoms more fragrant and sweeter to the taste. When first open, the blooms are but faintly tinged with pink, subsequently they deepen into a pale red, and stand up. When the period of flowering passes the heads droop and turn brown. The seed pods contain three or four seeds, which are kidney-shaped, and from dark green to violet color, and considerably smaller than the seeds of red clover.

This clover does not make much growth the first year, and attains full growth only in its third year. It yields less than the red clover, and has but little or no aftermath. It is hardier and sweeter than red clover, and being a perennial, is more lasting, and it makes a finer hay.

Wherever it has been tried, experience has taught that it is best to seed it down with red clover, or some grass, preferably orchard grass, for the reasons that it does not occupy the ground the first year, and is liable to fall and lodge badly if sown alone. I have noticed that it is much frequented by bees. It does not stand the long dry summers of our latitude well but seems to like cool, moist regions.

As compared with red clover, the hay is richer by two per cent in flesh formers—both cut in bloom. The analyses of both, as given by Professors Wolff and Knop, show :

Red clover:

Flesh formers	13.4
Heat producing substances	29.9
Crude fibre	35.8
Fat	3.2
Ash	6.2

Alsike:

Flesh formers	15.3
Heat producing substances	29.2
Crude fibre	30.5
Fat	3.3
Ash	8.3

. The great difference in the amount of crude fibre is noticeable, and shows decidedly in favor of Alsike clover.

SAPLING RED CLOVER—(*Trifolium erectum.*)

This is precisely the same plant as the common red clover, and is used in the same manner and for the same purposes. The only difference in it is, that the stems being stouter, it is not liable to lodge, but stand erect, and so be in a better condition to mow, and admits the sun to its roots better. As to which may be preferable is a mere matter of taste or prejudice. Either is good, the sapling clover being about two weeks later.

CRIMSON CLOVER—(*Trifolium incarnatum.*)

This is an annual, presenting a beautiful crimson flower when in bloom. It is principally valuable as a green food, though the hay is thought to be equal or superior to that made of red clover, but being an annual it interferes more with the operations of the farm, it being necessary to sow it as a separate crop.

An analysis of the hay cut in bloom, as made by Wolff and Knop, shows:

Flesh formers	12.2
Heating properties	30.1
Crude fibre	33.8
Fat	3.0
Ash	7.2

It is said to be earlier than lucerne or the common red clover. It may be sown upon wheat or grain stubble in the fall, the land being simply harrowed and the seed sown.

Few things, it is said, in the vegetable world, present a more beautiful sight than a field of crimson clover in full bloom. It is not grown to any extent in this State, a few bunches appearing sometimes in fields with other clover. Its chief value is in its quick return. Sown in autumn it may be mown early the succeeding spring, and so meet any scarcity of provender.

ALFALFA: LUCERNE—(*Medicago Sativa.*)

This is, beyond doubt, the oldest cultivated grass known, having been introduced into Greece from Media 500 B. C., and the Romans, finding its qualities good, cultivated it extensively, and by them it was carried into France when Cæsar reduced Gaul. It is emphatically a child of the sun, and revels in a heat that would destroy any other species of clover. But cold and moisture are hurtful to it. On the rich, sandy lands of the South it is invaluable, and will grow luxuriantly, making enormous yields of hay. Its nutritive constituents are almost identical with red clover, but it has one property not possessed by the latter, and that is, it is perennial. It does not stool as freely as red clover, and therefore must be sown rather thicker. It will contiune to furnish green pasturage later than red clover.

It does not grow well on any soil that has a hard pan, nor on thin soils. To secure a stand, the ground must be in a thorough state of tilth, well pulverized and mellow. A want of attention to this requisite has caused many to be disappointed in the result. But in well prepared, rich, gravelly or sandy loam, it succeeds remarkably, sending down its long tap-roots many feet into the subsoil, pumping up moisture from below, and thus will thrive when all other plants are drooping. In this respect it is far superior to clover. For the latter, a suitable surface soil is of equal importance with the subsoil, but for Lucerne a suitable subsoil is absolutely necessary, as the roots are not fibrous, only rootlets shooting off from the main tap-root. This tap root grows to be as large as a carrot. This enormous quantity of roots permeating the ground to the depth of several feet, necessarily prepares the land for increased production, the leguminous plants deriving the larger part of their sustenance from the atmosphere, and storing it in the roots ; so that, as a fertilizer, it stands deservedly high. The soil is not only fertilized to the amount of several tons per acre, but it is mellowed from the mechanical displacement of the soil and the admixture of decayed vegetable matter. As a prepartion for wheat it is equal to clover, and for corn better. Besides, a large amount of the leaves is necessarily strewn on the ground, and they shade it effectually.

The seed of Lucerne is yellow and heavy, when good. If brown, it has received too much heat in the mow, and if light colored, it indicates that it was saved too green. And the same precautions are necessary to be observed in regard to red clover. The time of sowing is the same with the other species of clover, that is, spring time. It should be sown in drills, and cultivated the first year, so as to keep down the weeds. It is easily smothered.

It derives its name, Alfalfa, from the Chilians. It grows spontaneously all over Chili, among the Andes, as well as on the pampas of that country, and of Buenos Ayres. The French and Spanish settlements of the Southern States adhere to it, and cultivate it in preference to all other forage plants. It would be a good addition to the farms of West Tennessee, especially in the sandy bottoms. It would also thrive upon the alluvial bottoms of any part of the State where the sun has fair play on the ground.

When properly managed, the number of cattle which can be kept in good condition on an area of Lucerne, during the whole season, exceeds belief. It is no sooner mown than it pushes out fresh shoots, and wonderful as the growth of clover sometimes is, in a field that has been lately mown, that of Lucerne is far more rapid. Lucerne will last for many years, shooting its roots—tough and fibrous almost at those of liquorice—downwards for nourishment, till they are altogether out of reach of drought. In the dryest and most sultry weather, when every blade of grass droops for want of moisture, Lucerne holds out its stem fresh and green as in the genial spring.

Although so luxuriant in France, it will not flourish in England for the want of sun. It has generally failed in the Northern States for the same reason, superadded to the cold, while in the South it is a fine, thrifty plant. It has been fully tested in Georgia and Alabama, and has given universal satisfaction. Horses there, it is said, require no other food when not constantly engaged in work. Five tons of good hay have been made to the acre. It is estimated that five horses may be supported during the entire year from one acre of it. It is ready for the mower a month before red clover, and springs up long before the usual pasture grasses. In saving it for hay, care must be exercised, as in red clover, not to expose the plant too long to the sun, as it will shrivel and dry up the leaves, and they will be lost. The time for cutting is when it is in full bloom, as in red clover.

Occasionally it is attacked by an insect, when it begins to turn yellow, then it should at once be cut, as it will quickly dry up otherwise. Owing to the scarcity of seed, and the small amount cultivated, it is quite expensive, but the farmer can test it on a small quantity of land, and at the same time secure seed for future sowing. The first year it is apt to be troubled by the presence of weeds, but these can be easily exterminated if the precaution is observed to run the mower over it before weeds go to seed. Afterwards no fears need be entertained on that subject.

This plant is well adapted to the use of persons living in small towns or villages, who have a small lot they wish to devote to hay for a single horse or cow. No other kind of clover or grass will equal it in quantity, while the quality is as good as the best.

On the whole, the farmers cannot do better than adopt the cultivation of this grass. It has proved, with all who have tested it, worthy of all the extravagant encomiums bestowed upon it.

An alalysis shows the hay to contain :

Flesh formers	14.4
Heating properties	22 5
Crude fibre	40.0
Fat	2.5
Ash	6.4

It will be seen that in flesh-forming constituents it surpasses red clover by one per cent.

SAINFOIN OR ESPARSETTE.—(*Onobrychis sativa.*)

Experiments have been made with this grass, and though so valuable in France as to be called sacred, it has not proved a success here. It requires two or three years to arrive at maturity, and during that time has to be watched closely, or it will be choked up with weeds or grasses. It does not yield as much hay as either red clover or lucerne, but is of a very superior kind, and is much vaunted as a good butter-making hay. It does not give cows the hoven, however much they may eat of it. Its seeds are also said to be superior to oats, and more nutritious, and are very fine for fowls, inciting them to lay. It does best on limestone soils, though succeeding well on gravelly or sandy land, and will stand a large amount of heat, though not much cold. It would probably suit the country further south better than Tennessee, though I have seen it growing in Stewart county, having been brought there by a Swiss family. It would probably grow on all our calcareous soils.

PASTURE GRASSES.

While there are over two hundred varieties of grasses cultivated in England for the use of domestic animals, in the occupied territory embraced within the United States there are not more than twenty-five; although there is a much greater diversity of soils, surface configuration, climate and latitude. The grasses constituting our meadows are nearly all derived from the eastern continent, where the abundance of the rich pasture lands teem with a great variety of nutritious herbage. All the cereals—oats, rye, wheat and barley, are indigenous to the old world. Indian corn is the greatest and almost the only valuable cereal contributed by the new world to the old. The great prairies east and west of the Mississippi abound in a charming and luxuriant vegetation, but the supply of food which they afford for the herds grazing upon them, in comparison to the overwhelming quantity of worthless herbage, is very scanty. Exactly the reverse is the condition of the pastures of the eastern hemisphere, where almost every plant that springs from the surface of the earth is rich in nutritive elements. The situation of Tennessee being midway between the East and West, partakes of both sections. We have in the State many thousands of acres of wild lands, situated not only on the mountain plateau, but on the highlands of the river lands, called with us "Barrens." These Barrens are covered with a dense growth of timber, and in some sections, where they have not been burned off, with undergrowth of various kinds. Where this undergrowth has been burned off by firing the leaves in the fall and winter, the pastures are as fine as are seen anywhere, not excepting the prairies. It is true there are many species of grasses that are worthless, or that are at least of doubtful value, yet enough of them exist there to make them invaluable to the stockgrower. In the fall of the year these grasses

4

become tall, will turn over and form a roof or covering to young grass that grows under them all the winter, and stock will paw at it until the covering removed, they get to the young succulent shoots thus kept alive throughout our short winters. A detailed description of these wild grasses, while it might interest the student, would be out of place in a work of this kind, intended to be entirely practical; for, however much they may be used in their indigenous situation, there is no probability of the farmer ever getting them transferred to his fields. The grasses we here treat of as pasture grasses, are alone those that will bear sowing in new situations, and to this class we will strictly adhere. For a more detailed description of the others, I refer the reader to the work sent out from this Bureau on the "Grasses of Tennessee."

With this explanation we will describe the subjoined.

NIMBLE WILL.—(*Muhlenbergia diffusa.*)

It is hardly necessary to do more than mention this grass, which forms, in many sections, the bulk of the pastures of the woods. It does not grow in fields, but in woods, where, in the fall, after rains have set in, it carpets the earth with living green. Various opinions are entertained as to its nutritive qualities. Some farmers contend that their stock are fond of it, and, on a sufficient range, cattle, horses and sheep will go into the winter sleek and fat from this vigorous grass. Others regard it as wellnigh worthless.

It freely propagates itself in all woods where the covering of leaves is not so great as to exclude the rays of the sun from the soil. Like other grasses, it does best on good lands, and the rich, black, loamy woods in many parts of the State are set with it.

It is said to be an excellent butter-making grass, and gives a particularly fine flavor to this article of food. It has never, to the knowledge of the writer, been sown, though, as it produces seed in a limited quantity, there is no reason why it should not be, if it is really a valuable grass.

BERMUDA GRASS.—SCOUTCH GRASS.—(*Cynodon dactylon.*)

Bermuda grass is a native of the West Indies, and is the principal grass of that torrid country. It has only lately been brought into notice as a valuable pasture grass for this State. In Louisiana, Texas and the South generally, it is, and has been the chief reliance for pasture for a long time, and the immense herds of cattle on the southern prairies subsist principally on this food. It revels on sandy soils, and has been grown extensively on the sandy hills of Virginia and North and South Carolina. From the extreme vitality of its long, rhizome roots, it is very difficult to eradicate when once it gets a good foothold. Occasionally the traveler meets with patches of Bermuda grass in the cotton fields of the South, and it is carefully avoided by the planter, any disturbance giving a new start to its vigorous roots. Some ditch around it, and others enclose it and let shrubbery do the work of destruction. It is used extensively on the southern rivers to hold the levees and the embankments of the roads. It is the only yard grass in that section. It forms a sward so tough it is almost impossible for a plow to pass through it. There is a saying in the South, " that it would take a team of six bull elephants to draw a thumb-lancet through it."

It will throw its runners over a rock six feet across, and soon hide it from view ; or, it will run down the sides of the deepest gully and stop its washing.

The parks of the South, set with it, present a very beautiful appearance if kept mown, and its pale green color acts as a great relief to the landscape when burning with the summer suns of the South. Hogs thrive upon its succulent roots, and horses and cattle upon its foliage. It has seed, but is always propagated by dropping cuttings in a furrow two or three feet apart, from the fact that the seed rarely mature, so that practically it may be said to have none. It, however, does not endure a shade, and the weeds must be mown from it the first year.

In some of the worn and gullied fields of Tennessee, on her mountain sides and on the sandy hills of many parts of the State, the cultivation of this grass would be a grand improvement, making the waste places to bloom, where now only sterility reigns. During the winter it, unlike blue-grass, disappears from view, but with the warming influences of the sun it springs up and affords a constant grazing through the spring, summer and autumn months. The farmers of the South, before the war, looked upon it as a curse rather than a blessing, and used every endeavor to destroy it. But a change of opinion has taken place in this respect, and it is encouraged in its growth.

It would be a good grass to mix with blue-grass, as, when it disappears in the winter, the blue-grass and white clover will spring up to keep the ground in a constant state of verdure. It grows luxuriantly on the top of Lookout Mountain, having been set there many years ago. This mountain is, 2,200 feet high, and has, as a matter of course, excessively cold winters ; so, if it thrives there, no fear need be entertained as to its capacity to endure our climate. Cattle are very fond of it, and will leave clover to feed upon Bermuda. It also has the capacity to withstand any amount of heat and drought, and months that are so dry as to check the growth of blue-grass, will only make the Bermuda greener and more thrifty. The experiment of mixing the two grasses, spoken of above has been tried with eminent success.

It is also used in the South as meadow grass, but Tennessee has so many other grasses of more value, that it would not be profitable to employ this, other than as a pasture grass.

Where it is indigenous, it has a great reputation as a fertilizer, and many fields so worn out as to be worthless, have been reclaimed by it. The labor of plowing it up is considerable, but the many improved plows of the present day would be easily dragged through it. There is a sacred grass in India called the Daub, and it is venerated by the inhabitants on account of its wonderful usefulness. This is said to be precisely the same as the Bermuda, except the changes made by the difference of climate and soil.

"Bermuda grass well set, which affords the finest and most nutritious pasturage I have ever seen, will keep almost any number of sheep to the acre—three or four times as many as blue-grass."

HAIRY MUSKIT—MEZQUITE—MESQUIT—(*Boulelova curtipendula.*)

Muskit 'grass has come into very general use in some parts of Virginia, North Carolina, and, to some extent, in Tennessee, and where used, has given much satisfaction. It is the grass of the northern and western prairies, and is very nutritious. In the absence of grasses better suited to this climate, the muskit might become a very popular grass, but such is not the case. Great quantities of it are annually cut and sold as prairie hay. It would be well for some enterprising farmer to experiment with it.

ANNUAL SPEAR GRASS—GOOSE GRASS—(*Poa annua.*)

This is one of the species of the valuable genus *poa* to which blue-grass belongs, and is a very common grass on all our swards,

and known as goose grass. It is so very like blue-grass that, to a
casual observer, it would be taken for it. But the florets are not
webbed, and in blue-grass the roots are creeping, while this is
tufted. It is a valuable grazing grass and sows itself. It is a common pasture grass of the Northern States, and is highly prized. It
flowers through the whole summer, unless dried up by a drought,
to which it easily yields. It forms the principle grazing of the
Unaka Mountains in Tennessee.

According to Prof. Way, this grass is less nutritious than blue-
grass when green, and more nutritious when dry.

WOOD MEADOW GRASS—(*Poa nemoralis.*)

This grass grows in moist, shady woods, is rank and luxuriant,
and is, like the other *poas*, greatly relished by stock. It will thrive
well in thickets and barrens, and is an early grass. It has been
treated of under the head of meadow grasses.

BLUE-GRASS—(*Poa pratensis.*)

This is the king of pasture grasses in the
Central Basin of Tennessee, and on soils
suited to its growth it is useless to attempt
the cultivation of any other kinds, except as
auxiliary to this. It is valuable both for
summer and winter pasturage, and no farmer occupying soils suited to its growth is
justifiable in being without it. It is easily
started, and the seeds are readily procured,
and once started, it is perennial. No
amount of pasturing is sufficient to destroy
it utterly, and, though eaten until no appearance of it is seen on the ground, with
rest for a few days, the earth is again car-
peted with its soft green foliage as luxuriantly as ever. " Whoever has blue-grass has
the basis for all agricultural prosperity, and
that man, if he has not the finest horses,
cattle and sheep, has no one to blame but
himself. Others in other circumstances may
do well, he can hardly help doing well if he
will try."

Its parentage is claimed by many States, and it is probably indigenous to some of them, though some authors say it was introduced from Europe. Let that be as it may, it grows readily in all parts of the United States north of latitude 40°, and lower down on suitable soils. It flowers in earliest summer, and gives a rich pasturage, except in the driest months, all the year. It varies in size in different localities, according to soil and climate. From the unexampled success its cultivation has met with in Kentucky, it has acquired the name of Kentucky blue-grass. The June or wire grass of the North is very much like it in general appearance, but the seed stalk is flattened, and for this reason the botanical name *poa compressa* is given. The seeds are not so fuzzy as those of the Kentucky blue-grass.

In all the middle portions of the United States it forms the principal constituent of the turf. In some sections it has been used as a hay, and from the analysis hereunto appended, it is full of all the constituents of nutrition. But it is not a success as a meadow grass, its chief excellence being exhibited as a pasture grass. It endures the frosts of winter better than any other grass we have, and if allowed to grow rank during the fall months, it will turn over and hide beneath its covering the most luxuriant of winter croppings. Many farmers pass their stock through the entire winter on it alone, feeding only when the ground is covered with snow.

As a lawn grass it stands pre-eminent among all others, its rich Paris green foliage, its uniform growth and its constant verdure making it beautiful both summer and winter.

A farm well set in blue-grass will yield at least ten dollars per acre in grazing, and yet men who have farms with all the constituents necessary to produce the best of grass will persistently wear them out in cultivation from year to year, with less net receipts by far than the yield of a pasture. In the work on Wheat Culture, issued from this office, it has been shown that a large proportion of Middle and East Tennessee abounds in limestone rocks, in fact, it underlies the Basin of Middle Tennessee and forms most of the foundations of the Eastern mountains. The blue-grass of Kentucky is made from soil produced by precisely the same strata of rocks seen here. Any farmer having land showing an outcrop of limestone with a grayish colored subsoil, may be assured he has the necessary soil. These rocks are looked upon as a curse, yet, without their presence, we could not have the magnificent parks of blue-grass seen around.

Blue-grass lands do not exist everywhere in the United States, and that should increase their value. They will be in demand, and that soon. The wild grasses that now are such an attraction to immigrants, on the table-lands of Tennessee, will ultimately be exhausted by the increase in population, while the demand for food and every variety of domestic animals will be proportionably augmented according to the increase of the population. Then every acre of land that will produce blue-grass will be in active demand, and will be devoted to stock raising, for which it is so well adapted, and sheep and cattle will then fleck every hillside.

The fame of the Kentucky blue-grass is so great that the majority of people suppose Tennessee cannot produce it so well, and they demand practical evidence of the fact. We have that very evidence here spread out before our eyes in the magnificent pastures of those who have adopted the proper management. Kentucky has famous pastures, because, in the outset of her cultivation of the blue-grass, a system of management was adopted that proved a success. That system has been thoroughly tested both in Kentucky and in some counties in Tennessee, and no one has made a failure who has attempted it. Those who have put themselves to the trouble of learning that system, and putting it in practice, have made as good grass as can be made in Kentucky or elsewhere. As in other crops, the quantity and quality of grass are in exact proportion to the care and management bestowed upon it, and the sod is as good, the blades as wide and long as can be seen anywhere, but this all depends on the skill and attention of the farmer. Some will sow a lot and then put in cattle, horses, sheep and hogs to keep it eaten to the ground throughout the year. Under such treatment the grass disappears, and such farmers conclude their soils are not adapted to grass. Let the grass get a vigorous start, protect it from stock for the first year, and fertilize it with stable manure, or some of the superphosphates, and be sure not to overcrowd the pasture with stock. This is the true secret of having good pastures.

Dr. F. H. Gordon, of Smith county, spent years in studying the habits of blue-grass, and finally succeeded in giving the best instructions for securing a stand: •

"Some seventy years ago," he says, writing in 1871, "two

young men named Cunningham came from the south branch of the Potomac, in Virginia, to Strode's creek, in Bourbon county, Kentucky. They had studied and practiced the blue-grass system on the Potomac. They jointly purchased two hundred acres of land on Strode's creek, and sowed the whole tract in timothy and blue-grass. In a few years their whole tract was covered with a luxuriant coat of grass. They had brought with them the seed, on a pack horse, all the way from Virginia. Their farm soon attracted the attention of their neighbors who began to visit, and learn how to manage grass. In 1835 I, too, went to see the Cunninghams and many other farmers in the blue-grass region, in order to learn the system. I devoted many weeks to the study of the system—going with the best farmers over their farms and seeing their management, asking many questions and writing down their answers. Then, the Cunninghams, like many others, had grown to be wealthy on the profits of the blue-grass. One of them, Robert, then had two thousand acres in blue-grass and Isaac had three thousand. Nearly all the farmers I visited owed the luxury of their blue-grass to the direct instruction of the Cunninghams. To me it was a feast to travel over and view the fine sod of grass on the first two hundred acres which had caused the whole blue-grass region to become so beautiful, prosperous and wealthy.

While learning the blue-grass system, I saw in every neighborhood that those who had studied the system closest had the best pastures invariably. You can see in all that region of blue-grass some farms where all the lots look like some of ours in Tennessee, which are gnawed all the year round by calves, sheep and geese. This is because the owner does not think enough about its management. He does all the work and incurs all the expense necessary to make the richest pastures, and then wastes it all by bad and thoughtless management. But there are some farmers in almost every county in Tennessee who well understand the Kentucky system. Those who intend to sow grass may learn the system from them. What a scene of comfort, beauty, luxury and wealth, will this whole Middle Tennessee present, when it shall be covered with the richest blue-grass! Such will be the future of this fine country."

"Blue-grass will always pay a good profit. Every acre set in it will pay its taxes and a good profit besides. We now till too much land. We ought to till less and make more grass. Let not an acre be idle. There is our true interest. Cotton, tobacco, rice, hemp and sugar need laborers, but grass does not. If we **sow our** lands in grass we can do without so much labor. The indisposition of farmers to take advantage of experience is shown in the following case, which is in point:

"I know a rocky lot of about six acres which I myself sowed in 1835. During last year (1870) it afforded a profit to the present owner of full $10 per acre. The owner has no grass on the balance of his land, and does not intend to have any. He has lived during his whole life in sight of rich pastures of blue grass, and knows that his whole tract will produce as good grass as those pastures, yet he will not sow grass. The reader will say that this farmer, with his six rocky acres of blue-grass, is a singular man. But he is not very singular, because hundreds of farmers here know just as well the value of blue-grass as he does, and yet they do not sow it.

It is generally conceded that the lands most productive of blue-grass are the calcareous soils. Lime is a natural stimulant to it, and it flourishes best where natural supplies of this salt are found. Go into a pasture that has an occasional out-cropping of limestone, and the sprigs of grass surrounding the rocks will be found more luxuriant than anywhere else. Our lower silurian formation then, wherever found, may be safely sown in this grass. The Basin of Middle Tennessee, and the valleys of East Tennessee, are all well suited for this grass, and I have seen some good sods in Carroll county, West Tennessee. It also grows upon many places amongst the hills of the rivers, though not so luxuriantly as in the black loams of the silurian and devonian formations. Lime, though a great stimulant to its growth, is not an essential ingredient in the soil. Blue grass will always grow well under walnut and locust trees.

We have in Middle and East Tennessee the same character of soil that exists in the blue-grass country of Kentucky, and, owing to our milder climate, can produce a better winter pasturage than can be produced in the colder climate of Kentucky. Little land exists in Tennessee but what will produce this grass profitably.

Select the lot to be sown, and clean off all brush, leaves and briars. If it cannot be done with a stalk-rake, use hand-rakes, as the seed must come in contact with the soil. Seed sown on a bed of leaves will soon germinate, but the rootlets, being unable to burrow in the soil, will quickly parch up and die. If the land is thickly covered with trees it will not thrive well, therefore it is necessary the timber should be thinned out. Leave the tallest trees that are really the more valuable, taking off the low, bushy kinds that make too much shade. It is an admitted fact that blue-grass does better in partial shade than where there is none. It does not endure a drought as well as some other grasses, and, conse-quently, some degree of shade is essential to protect it from the scorching rays of midsummer.

So many seasons have been recommended as the proper time of sowing, that it may be said each one, under favorable circumstances, is a good time. One Kentucky farmer says: "Any time in the winter, when snow is on the ground, sow broadcast from three to four quarts of seed to the acre. With the spring the seeds germinate, and are very fine and delicate in the sprouts. No stock should be allowed for the first year, nor until the grass seeds in June for the first time the second year. The best plan is to turn on the stock when the seeds ripen in June. Graze off the grass, then allow the fall growth and graze all winter, taking care never to feed the grass closely at any time."

Another authority says: "Follow nature and obey her dictates. The seeds ripen in June, and are scattered by the winds and rains as soon as ripe, therefore sow the seeds as soon as they can be gathered."

This plan might be a proper one in a colder or moister climate than ours, but here it would result in the grass being often dried up by the droughts that are almost invariable in the latter part of summer.

Many sow, as stated in the above quotation, on winter snows, and that is a very good plan, but care should be observed to have the ground free from leaves before the snow falls.

There are others who sow in the latter part of February or the first of March, and this sometimes does as well as any, provided time is given for the grass to get sufficient hold to resist the wither-ing effects of the summer's drought. The main care to be taken is to get the grass large enough to live through freezing or dry weather. It will resist the effects of frost better than heat, however, and, taking this into consideration, the most approved time of sowing is in the latter part of August or first of September. If sown at this time the autumnal rains will germinate the seed, and besides, at this season, there is comparatively little trash on the ground, the leaves having not yet fallen. The ground being prepared, the seeds are sown broadcast, at the rate of one bushel per acre, and the sower should be followed with a harrow, or, if the ground is very loose, with a stiff brush. This will give them a sufficient covering. It is a fact, demonstrated by actual experiment, as shown in one of the tables herein contained, that grass seeds will vegetate best at a depth of one-quarter of an inch. It may be supposed that, with no more covering than will be given by a harrow or brush, a great many seeds will be uncovered. This is very true, but in one pound of blue-grass seeds (clean seed) there are 3,888,000 seeds. By a computation every square inch of surface contains from ten to twelve seeds. With this amount on the surface, one scarcely need fear a stand, when, if one or two take root, there will be in a year an excessively close turf.

There can be but little difference of opinion in regard to the treading of stock after sowing. All writers and farmers agree that for one year, at least, it should be kept from all stock. After that there is some difference.

Dr. Gordon, who, as before stated, paid more attention to it than any one else in the State, adopted a plan of management that has been repeatedly tested, with uniform success. It was this:

He sowed, either in the autumn or spring months, indiscriminately, as suited his convenience. He usually sowed with rye, wheat or barley, if sowed in an open field, but if in a woods lot, he sowed with rye, or after a crop of millet. At any rate, the soil must be well cleaned off and broken up, as well as the nature of the land permits, then, after the grain is sown the land is harrowed, and if possible rolled. After this the grass seeds were sown and brushed lightly. Immediately afterward, all the cattle, horses and sheep were turned in that could be secured. If there was not enough on his place he borrowed his neighbor's stock, and let them run on it until the ground was well packed all over the surface, and then, and not until then, were they removed. If after millet (and that is greatly recommended, as it destroys more effectively than anything else all weeds), harrow about the first of September thoroughly, sow the seed, brush as before, and then turn on the stock. If it is desired to sow in the spring, in the latter part of February or early in March; if not practicable sooner, harrow the grain field, the ground having been well prepared in the fall sowing, sow the seed and then turn stock on the wheat, rye or barley, as the case may be. Oat land may be sown in the same way. The treading of the stock packs in the seeds and prevents the grass from drying up in the summer heats, or freezing out in frosts. Dr. Gordon considered an open, loose, porous surface to be unfavorable to the safety of the young grass, but if packed as directed, the grass will spring quickly up, get a firm hold, and the loose condition of the sub-soil will favor the transmission of the roots to a good depth.

The after treatment is simple, and that is to allow no stock on during the first year, but as soon as the seed stalks begin to shoot up the next year, pasture it so closely that it cannot go to seed.

Dr. Gordon differs in this respect from other authors, who allow it to seed one time for purposes stated below. He would not let it seed at all. His great success in this branch of agriculture will, in every place where he is known, give weight to his authority.

Others say no stock should go on it for at least two years, or at least until after the first seeding, which will take place in June of the second year. Some of the best blue-grass lots in Middle Tennessee have been started by following either of the above plans. Of one thing there cannot be a doubt, and that is the ground should not be well broken up. On the surface it should be as firmly packed as possible to secure a perfect stand, and form a perfect turf. When the surface is too loose, the grass easily dries up and is much easier frozen out, the seeds not going into a germinating depth. Under favorable weather, seed sown in the spring on a crop of oats will do as well as fall sowing. What is meant by favorable weather is that no unusual dry weather supervenes. But there is always the risk of meeting with unfavorable weather in spring sowing, and on that account we would recommend sowing in autumn. But it is better the sowing should take place as early in the fall as the weather will permit, or, indeed, the latter part of summer, if there is a proper degree of moisture in the soil. Some farmers sow a limited amount of seed daily, and over the same surface sprinkle shelled corn, then turn on their hogs. They root in search of the corn, and thus plant the seed, doing the work of plow and harrow.

This, to say the least, is a slovenly plan, and though possibly securing a good stand, the ground is so roughened it can never make a beautiful pasture.

If the land is loose, as some soils are, it will answer a very good purpose to scratch up the surface well with a sharp-toothed harrow, and this is especially the case where the roots of undergrowth exist to a great extent.

AFTER TREATMENT.

Of one fact there cannot be a doubt, and in this lies the whole secret of having remunerative pastures of blue grass; and that is do not pasture it to death. It is true it will stand almost unlimited grazing, but there is a point beyond which it will cease to be profitable, and that limit should never be passed. The better plan is to have the lots divided, and allow the stock on one until it is cropped down, and then, when no longer any pickings can be taken from it, do not allow the stock to continue to tread it, simply to have them on a grass lot. It will not only do the stock no good, but, by constant tramping, the grass is unable to throw up any foliage, and in time it will die, for the roots must draw some nourishment from the atmosphere, or they will perish. Allow the grass to recuperate by changing the stock from one pasture to another, and *never overstock it.* Grass that will keep ten oxen in growing order will fatten five oxen quickly. Stock of all kinds are constant feeders, and there should always be forage enough to enable them to get plenty to eat without the labor of hunting for it.

There is much variety of opinion on the amount of stock that ought to be put on an acre. This arises from the difference in the capacity of the land, some soils, being rich, dry and porous, will stand much heavier grazing than others. It is safer to err on the safe side, and it is better to put in too few than too many. If stock are fattened quickly, they are more remunerative than when fattened slowly. Then, when one lot is sold out, they can be replaced by others. Ordinarily, two acres of grass are requisite for one three-year-old ox, and what will fatten one ox will fatten ten head of sheep.

Blue-grass should be allowed to go to seed once or twice, or until the ground is well set or turfed over, and then never more. It is a grass that propagates itself by its creeping roots or rhizomes, and it is the disposition of all plants and animals to lose vitality in the process of reproduction.

Though perennial, its vitality may be greatly lowered by the effort of reproduction, so that it may lie dormant for some time afterward, before starting again its vigorous growth. Stock should be kept out at seeding time, or before, in fact, so as not to eat down the seed stalks.

It sometimes happens that dry weather sets in during the summer months, and the grass becomes so dry it will burn. Still stock will greedily eat it. The grass having dried full of nourishing juices, it is equal to the best of hay, and stock will still fatten upon it.unless the dried grass has been drenched with rains.

The fall growth of some lots should be kept untouched by stock, and in this way a fine winter pasturage will be secured. The grass will get high enough to fall over and protect the surface foliage, and stock will keep up their flesh on it during the winter without feed. When snows fall, cattle will require to be fed, but horses, mules and sheep will paw off the snow, unless it is too deep, and get at the grass. It is the first deciduous plant that puts forth its leaves in the spring. Good fat lambs can be sent into the market earlier than from any other grass. It makes milk rich in butter, and gives the latter a fine golden color, without changing its taste, or, like clover, imparting its peculiar flavor to it.

The following is an analysis of this grass, as compared with some other well known grasses. (Way.)

FIRST.—DRIED AT A TEMPERATURE OF 212°.

100 PARTS OF	Flesh Forming Principles.	Fatty Matters.	Heat Producing Principles.	Woody Fibre.	Ash.
Blue-grass give	10.35	2.63	43.06	38.02	5.94
Timothy	11.36	3.55	53.35	26.46	5.28
Orchard grass	13.53	3.14	44.32	33.70	5.31
Clover	22.55	3.67	44.47	19.75	9.56
White clover	18.76	4.38	40.04	26.53	10.29
Sweet scented vernal	10.43	3.41	43.48	36.36	6.36

SECOND.—AS TAKEN FROM THE FIELD IN BLOSSOM.

WITHOUT DRYING, 100 PARTS OF	Water.	Flesh Forming Principles.	Fatty Matters.	Heat Producing Principles.	Woody Fibre.
Blue-grass give	67.14	3.41	0.86	14.15	12.49
Orchard grass	70.00	4.06	0.94	13 30	10.11
Timothy	57.21	4.86	1.50	22.85	11.32
Red clover	81.01	4.27	0.96	8.45	3.76
White clover	79.71	3.80	0.89	8 14	5.38
Sweet scented vernal	80.35	2.05	0.67	8.54	7.15

There is, in all pastures, a number of bare spots that seem to resist the efforts of blue-grass to sod. By mixing other seeds with the blue-grass, these spots can be made to produce as well as other places. In a natural meadow, by careful counting, several species are often found growing intimately on every inch of earth. On a good natural pasture in one square foot of sod, there have been counted 1,000 plants, consisting of twenty distinct species. This is nature's own arrangement, and may be safely copied. In such a pasture not an inch of surface is unoccupied. It may be thought an inch or two here and there makes but little difference in the space occupied. But every blade of grass is of some importance, and it is astonishing the aggregate of these barren places.

Now, once more, let it be urged on the farmers of Tennessee to look into this matter of pastures, and provide themselves with this highly important adjunct to every farm. No home is complete without pastures, and yet there are many who will depend either upon the fortuitous wild grasses for grazing, or feed their stock from the crib all through the year. With a rich blue-grass lot, no stock need be fed, except while at work; and, indeed, it is sometimes the case that in dry, scarce years, crops have been made with horses and mules that had no other provender than a blue-grass lot.

SHEEP'S FESCUE—(*Festuca ovina*—*Perennial.*)

The fescue grasses are very popular in New England, and grow well in Tennessee, having been introduced in some localities. They are perennial, and grow in tufts, and from their profuse foliage they form excellent pasturage for cattle, and especially for sheep, hence the name of one variety. Mixed with other grasses the sheep's fescue would be a good addition to our native grasses. It would be especially useful on dry hill-sides, or sandy, old fields, where blue-grass will not thrive well. It has long leaves, and they are much sought for by cattle. It has been grown extensively in East Tennessee, and is grown in some localities in Davidson county, without much success. The Hon. Staunton Gould says this grass forms the great bulk of the sheep pastures of the Highlands of Scotland, where it is the favorite food of the sheep, and where the shepherds believe it to be more nutritious for flocks than any other. Gmelin says the Tartars choose to encamp during the summer where this grass is most abundant, because they believe it to be the most wholesome for all cattle, but especially for sheep. Linnæus asserts that sheep have no relish for hills and heaths without it. It grows in dry sandy soils, where all other vegetation parches up. The roots are long, turf short and dense, making it well suited for lawns. It retains its verdure during the most extended droughts. It will not bear maturing, for then it is dispossessed by other grasses. Its great value is for pasturage upon sandy soils. It will suit the Cumberland Table-land. The Woburn experiments showed that, cut at the time of flowering, the product of one acre was 5,445 pounds, which gave 212 pounds of nutritive matter. The same number of pounds was obtained, cut when the seeds were ripe, but there were only 127 pounds of nutritive matter. The aftermath yielded 3,403 pounds of hay, having 66 pounds of nutritive matter. From this it appears that there is a difference between the results obtained by chemists and practical feeders as to its nutritive properties.

MEADOW FESCUE—RANDALL GRASS—EVERGREEN GRASS
—(*Festuca pratensis.*)

This grass has received some attention in different parts of the State, and has met with a warm reception from those testing it. It ripens its seed long before any other grass, and, consequently, affords a very early nip to cattle. It has been raised under various names, in Virginia, as "Randall Grass," in North Carolina as "Evergreen Grass." In the mountain lands of Virginia, a writer says: "The variety of forage best adapted to sheep-grazing on the mountain lands is the 'Randall,' a tall, coarse grass, growing freely on the rocky soil to a height of six feet, remaining green and affording fine herbage all the winter."

Mr. James Taylor, writing to the Agricultural Bureau from North Carolina, says:

"The evergreen grass is very good for pasturing through the fall and winter. I have no knowledge of its origin. It will do best when sown on dry land, and is well adapted to sheep. It grows well on rocky soil, to the height of four or five feet when ripe, continuing green in the spring, and affording fine herbage throughout the winter. It is best to sow in the spring with oats. A peck of well cleaned seed is enough for an acre, or a bushel in the chaff. It ripens about the first of June, or a little before rye harvest, and is cut with scythe and cradle as we cut rye."

TALL FESCUE GRASS—(*Festuca elatior.*)

This is a variety of the same, naturalized from Europe, and suited to a rich loam, such as is found in the Central Basin. The Woburn experiments show it to yield more nutritious matter per acre, when cut in flower, than any other grass, cut either in flower or seed. The number of pounds obtained was 51,046, which weighed, when dry, 17,866 pounds, loss in drying, 33,180 pounds and furnished 3,988 pounds of nutritive extract.

There are several other fescue grasses, as the Spiked Fescue, (*F. loleacea*), Hard Fescue, (*F. duriuscula*), and the Nodding Fescue (*F. utans*), all indigenous to this country. The last two are good hay grasses, as well as the Meadow Fescue. The Hard Fescue was analyzed by Way and found to contain water, 69.33 ; flesh-formers, 3.70; fat, 1.02; heat-producers, 12.46; woody fibre, 11.83; ash, 1.66. The Woburn experiments gave as the produce of one acre, 18,376 pounds, cut in flower; loss in drying 10,116 pounds; nutritive matter, 1,004 pounds. Cut in seed, the produce weighed 19,075 pounds, loss in drying, 10,481 pounds, leaving nutritive extract, 446 pounds. It grows well on a sandy loam. The seeds weigh ten pounds to the bushel.

TALL MEADOW OAT GRASS—(*Arrhenatherum avenaceum.*)

This grass is very popular in France, from whence it was introduced, and is there known by the name of "Ray Grass."

It will grow well on any land that produces clover. Its limit is about 1,500 feet above the sea. It grows quickly and forms a very excellent grass for early pasturage, probably earlier than any other. It is mown down for hay, and, after cutting, it throws up a perfect mat of aftermath, that will yield an extremely rich pasture. It was only introduced into Tennessee a few years ago, and it has received extravagant praises, as is usual with new introductions.

It succeeds well in West Tennessee, and will probably suit that locality better than any other grass, except Herd's grass. It would form a good grass to mix with others, such as timothy, Herd's grass, clover or bluegrass.

The analysis of the hay by Way, is as follows: Flesh-formers, 12.95; fatty matters, 3.19; heat-producing principles, 38.03; woody fibre, 34.24; mineral matters, 11.59.

This shows it to rank as a nutritious grass, among the best of the meadow grasses, and almost equal to any of the pasture grasses, though it is said cattle and sheep do not like to be confined to it alone. The produce from an acre from Mr. Sinclair's experiments at Woburn, was 17,015 pounds; loss in drying 11,635 pounds; nutritive matter, 664 pounds. Cut when the seeds were ripe the weight was 16,335 pounds; loss in drying, 10,617 pounds; nutritive matter, 255 pounds. Weight of aftermath, 13,612 pounds; nutritive matter of which was 265 pounds.

SWEET-SCENTED VERNAL GRASS—(*Anthoxanthum odoratum.*)

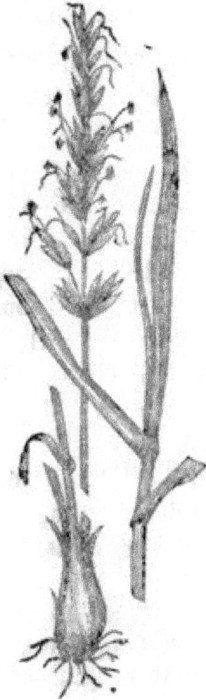

This grass was introduced from Europe, and possesses rather poor qualities as a pasture grass, as neither sheep nor cattle relish it. It is early, however, and hardy. It is one of the first as well as one of the last grasses that appear. Its nutritive qualities are said to exist to a much larger extent in the fall than in the spring, and greater when cut at maturity than in bloom. It has a mixture of benzoic acid among its constituents, which imparts to it a highly aromatic character, and this is so strong that other grasses with which it may be mixed are affected by it. It is not in general use in Tennessee, but would probably add to the value of pastures if sown with other grasses. Cows running on it are, by some, said to give a rich milk and highly flavored butter, but Mr. Gould thinks this is an error. It may be known by rubbing its green leaves in the fingers, to which it yields its scent. On certain soils favorable to its growth, it will root out almost every other kind and take complete possession. Its seeds have a spiral awn, and when taken in the hand, affected by its moisture, the awns will uncoil, and the seeds will appear to move as insects. There are six or seven pounds in a bushel, and nine hundred and twenty-three thousand two hundred in a pound. Its analysis, according to Way, ranks it, when dry, a litttle higher than blue-grass, as follows: Flesh-formers, 10.43; fatty matters, 3.41; and heat producing principles, 43.48. Blue-grass gives, flesh-formers, 10.35; fat, 2.63; heat-producers, 43.06.

The best test of all grasses is their effects upon animals. If animals thrive and fatten upon any grass, and that grass is perennial, hardy and durable, it is a good pasture grass; otherwise not, whatever individual experiments in the laboratory may indicate. We know that stock of all kinds eat blue grass voraciously and thrive upon it; we know, also, that they do not like the *anthoxanthum*. Both are alike hardy and durable. Therefore the blue-grass, upon suitable soils, is to be preferred, whatever chemical research may determine.

WHITE CLOVER—(*Trifolium repens.*)

White clover has been lauded to the skies by some, and by others depreciated as a vile weed. It is beyond question, next to blue-grass, one of our most valuable grazing plants. Its analysis shows it to be equal to red clover in most respects, and superior as a fat producing plant.

It is to the pasture what red clover is to the meadow, and is a suitable food not only for cattle and horses, but for hogs. They thrive amazingly on it. After the first flowering it salivates horses, but has no such effect upon cattle or sheep. As a honey-producing flower, the white clover is not surpassed by any plant, the florets, some years, being almost full of syrup.

It varies very much in different years, sometimes almost disappearing, then again, another year, being thick in every pasture. So much is this the case, that we have what are called "white clover years." This is due to the presence or absence of rain. When there is a wet spring white clover appears in great luxuriance every-where, and in dry weather it only shows itself in abundance on moist lands.

It is indigenous to both Europe and the United States, and, though growing everywhere here, it has to be sown on the Northern pastures. Here it comes spontaneously, almost taking every other grass, and sometimes destroying other grasses. It is an invaluable accompaniment of blue grass, especially triumphant where the blue-grass is pastured too heavily.

The comparative value of white and red clover, cut in bloom, may be seen by the following analyses by Prof. Way:

CLOVERS.	Water.	Flesh formers.	Fat.	Heaters.	Woody fibre.	Ash.
Red clover.............................	81.01	4.27	.69	8.45	3.76	1.82
White clover.............................	79.71	3.80	.89	8.14	6.38	2.08

JAPAN CLOVER OR KING GRASS.—*Lespedeza striata.)*

It has been but a few years since this plant has been brought to notice in this country, though its existence was mentioned as early as 1784 by Thunberg, a German chemist, who saw it growing in Japan. About the year 1849 it was noticed in the vicinity of Charleston, S. C., the seeds having been brought probably from Japan or China in tea boxes. A short while afterwards it was discovered at a distance of forty miles from Charleston, and still later near Macon, Ga.

Within the last six years it has developed itself in many of the counties of this State, especially in Henderson and Warren, where it is covering all old fields, and in many instances rooting out broom grass and other grasses, showing itself well worthy of the name given it by Mr. Pendleton, of king grass.

It seems especially adapted to the Southern States, not flourishing above 36°, growing with great luxuriance on the poorest soils, and retaining vitality in its roots in the severest droughts. It is said to be a fine plant for grazing, and being perennial in warm climates, needs no re-sowing and but little attention. On soils unfit for anything else, it furnishes good pasture and supplies a heavy green crop for turning under and improving the land. It cannot stand severe cold, and in high latitudes cannot be depended on as a good pasture grass, although it comes up and supplies an abundant forage for a few months. It should be sown in January or February in the Southern States, and about one bushel of seed to ten acres is required to secure a good stand the first year. It is said to be an excellent renovator of old fields, and to bring them up to a high degree of fertility in an incredibly short space of time.

Mr. E. M. Pendleton, of Georgia, speaking of it, says: "I am willing to concede to it several things that do not apply to any other plant we have ever grown in this latitude:

1. "It grows on poor land with more luxuriance than any other grass or weed I have ever seen; and as it has a small leaf, rather contravenes the general idea of vegetable physiologists, that large-leaved plants feed mostly on the atmosphere. I suppose, however, that this deficiency is counteracted to a large extent by the number of leaves, for they are legion.

2. "It has great powers of endurance, so far as the roots are concerned; but the branches and leaves will parch and die out

under a burning sun very soon, especially where it grows sparsely.
During a wet summer it luxuriates wherever propegated on poor
hill-sides as well as meadow lands. It loves, however, rainy
seasons on thirsty lands, and I fear will not prove to be all we desire
in such localities. It, however, reminds us of an anecdote of Mr.
Dickson, when he was showing some gentlemen his farm during
the prevalence of a severe drought. As they passed through a
cornfield in which some of the stalks were actually dying for lack
of moisture, one of them called his attention to several in that condition. "Yes," said he, "I perceive the fact—but *it dies game.*"
And so of the Japan clover, it dies from severe drought, but rallies
again as soon as the rain sets in.

3. "It is a good pasturage for stock, and I think would make
good hay, if cut and cured. This I intend to test the present
season. But I do not believe that our stock like it as well as the
native grasses, and doubt whether it is as nutritious as the Bermuda. As cattle love variety, however, this may subserve a good
purpose in that way. My opinion, however, is, from not very close
observation in the matter, that they would soon tire out on it exclusively.

4. "It furnishes a large supply of vegetable matter to the soil,
and I belive will prove to be the best humus making plant we
have at the South, where so much is needed from our clean cotton
culture. As it is said to be difficult to gather the seed in large
quantities, I intend to plow up the surface where it has seeded, and
rake up the grass and top soil, and sow this dirt over my oat and
wheat fields, and especially on the poor places. My opinion is that
a most luxuriant growth of this clover will follow, which can be
turned under in the fall while green, and thus furnish not only
humus but nitrogen to the soil.

5. "Another rare quality of this plant is indicated in the name I
have given it—king grass—in the fact that it absolutely roots out
and destroys every living plant in its widespread path. Not even
old Bermuda, which has so long held undisputed sway over his cir-
cumscribed fields, can resist its encroaches. I have a bottom long
since given up to the Bermuda. Recently I passed through it and
found that the Lespedeza had almost completely throttled it, though
like Mr. Dickson's corn, *it died game,* as here and there, peering
above its enemy, could be seen an isolated sprig of Bermuda, which,

as it cannot stand shade, will have to yield entirely before the close of another season. I have but little doubt that any pest like coco or Bermuda could be rooted out by this *king grass* in a few years in any locality, and would recommend it to be sown on such fields if for no other purpose. I intend to give it a fair trial myself on one or two similar localities."

In like manner the Hon. H. W. Ravenel, of South Carolina, regards it with great favor, and thinks its timely appearance will be ultimately a source of great wealth to the people of the Southern States. Many places that were regarded as worthless before its appearance, are now made profitable as a pasture, with the aid of this grass.

Mr. Samuel McRamsey, of Warren county, says this clover made its appearance in that locality in 1870. It is fast covering the whole country. It supplies much grazing from the first of August until frost. It is short; but very hardy. Sheep are very fond of it, and cattle will eat it. It is killing out the broomsedge wherever it appears. It grows exceedingly well on red clay, and with a little care covers red hillsides that are much too common all over the State. If it will do this and destroy the broom grass, it should be cultivated. It is not good for meadow and is only valuable for pasture.

The Hon. M. T. Polk considers it almost worthless for grazing, having made many experiments with it. His opinion is entitled to great weight.

MANAGEMENT OF MEADOWS,

AND

CONCERNING MANURES.

Meadows exist in various sections of the State to a limited extent, and it being the object of this work to foster this branch of agriculture the best plans for encouraging and treating them will be discussed. The subject requires no argument to encourage it, as every right-thinking man will see at a glance the great importance of growing more hay. It is, in the observation of every one, that vast amounts of baled hay are brought by rail and river from those States already embarked in the cultivation of grasses. While we have the best climate in the United States for this purpose, as already stated, we have a soil unparalleled for fertility, and well suited to almost all varieties of grasses described, and, besides, being on the border of the cotton States, we have a market at our doors for our surplus.

If we do this our country will assume such a charming appearance that it will delight the eye of every passenger who travels through it on the many lines of railroads, besides repaying the owners all the care bestowed on it. Our citizens are not so much to blame for this backwardness in the cultivation of the grasses as would appear at first sight. The routine established before the war was hard to break up, but they are looking around for some more profitable method of farming. To establish meadows is the part of wisdom. Just how to do this we propose to tell here as fully as our space will permit. We shall consider:

1st. The preparation of meadow lands.

2nd. Selection of suitable seeds for sowing and method of mixing.

3rd. Times of sowing and the best methods of securing stands.

4th. Cutting, curing and storing the hay.

5th. Improvement of meadows.

6th. Manures and manner of their application.

PREPARATION OF MEADOW LANDS.

This is of the utmost importance when we reflect that any want of attention to all the details necessary to insure success involves a considerable loss, not only in money and labor, but also in the length of time required to undo and correct the error. God sows the pastures to our hands, but man must sow the meadows. A man may think he is pursuing the most judicious course possible, but he may be in error, and an honest mistake does not free the farmer from loss. He must inform himself correctly on the character of the land to be sown, and then, with every facility at his command, acquaint himself with the grasses best adapted to its requirements.

In the first place, though many varieties of grass will grow well on moist land, it is not to be understood that they will thrive best on wet lands. When the water stands on the surface all the year, the character of the hay is nearly worthless, being full of moisture and with but little nutritive principles in it. Consequently it is very important to have soils properly drained, if they require it. It will largely increase the quantity and greatly improve the quality of the crop. With the soil full of moisture it becomes sour, and, though full of fertility, it is unavailable to the plant. With wet soil, it is impossible to put the land in a proper state of tilth. So all things point to the necessity of drainage.

It may be proper to state that every piece of ground on which water will stand two hours after a rain, will be benefitted by a system of drainage. This seems to the Southerner to be such a stupendous undertaking that nearly every one is discouraged from making the effort. When it is supposed that draining can only be effected by ditching in every direction, and laying great stretches of pipes, the undertaking does seem indeed to be very costly.

The method of pipe-laying is the best, and as our farmers see the good effects of a cheaper method, they will gradually, and by slow degrees, come to practice the more substantial methods. A

Northern land owner does not hesitate to spend fifty or seventy-five dollars on a single acre, when he can bring into cultivation a choice piece of bottom. But the Hollanders surpass every other people on earth in this particular. Nearly every foot of land they own has been reclaimed from the sea by a system of dykes, levees and ditches. Their lands being lower than the water courses that run through them, their only resource is to lift the watters that are collected in the ditches by means of steam pumps. This is done, it is true, at the expense of the public, but the farmers pay an annual tax to keep it up, or they would soon be flooded by the accumulating waters that penetrate the soil from every side.

There are many methods of draining land, but we will confine ourselves to the method of doing it as effectually as the Dutch, but at such an expense that even a renter can afford it, for the increase of one year's crop. A German gardner of New York leased ten acres of land that proved to be boggy, and the first three years his crops, in spite of all the attention he could give them, barely paid rent and support him. He was advised to try draining, and although but seven years were left of his lease, he did it at a cost of $500. The result fully justified the expense, for in the remaining seven years he made, over and above all expenses, money enough to pay $12,000 for the farm he had drained. No land can produce well without the aid of heat and proper aeration. If the soil is full of water it will be impervious to the air, and the water will also counteract the effects of the sun's rays, and the ground will be cold and lifeless. Without the influence of heat and air, necessary chemical changes in the constituents of the soil cannot take place, consequently the roots fail to find the nourishment they are seeking —they fail to penetrate the soil to a sufficient depth, and instead of a rich subsoil, there will only be surface soil to support vegetation. That soon becomes exhausted, and the land appears worn out. Draining opens up a mine of fertilizers below, the roots run quickly down to it, and there is no question that the crops are greatly increased. There is much land in our State that would be greatly improved by draining. The soils that will be improved can be ascertained, during the wet season, by digging a hole in the fields and watching the height to which the water rises. In many places it will remain almost on a level nearly all winter; in others showing itself one, two or three feet below it. And this, too, on rolling lands that are supposed to be dry enough. Not only are the wet lands made dryer, but the dry lands made wetter. This is effected by the soil becoming porous, so as to better admit the moisture of rains and dews. It is made warmer, and consequently frosts will have less effect, there being less moisture to freeze on the surface. And besides, by being warmer the crops come on earlier.

Our northern farmers practice almost exclusively tile draining. This is a costly mode, and if it were the only way our farmers would be frightened at once from the effort. But so thoroughly is this plan practiced, that it is no longer an experiment. Some counties in Ohio have spent the public funds in digging and draining the mains, so that farmers can lay their drains into them. Wood county, Ohio, in 1867, spent in one year $500,000 in digging mains. One drain was dug thirty miles long, and six feet deep, while the districts dug four hundred miles more.

The Agricultural College of Michigan, appointed a committee to investigate the effects of draining. They bought twenty-five acres of swampy land, covered with bog-grass, rushes, flags and other worthless vegetation. They laid about 800 yards of tiles at an expense of $480, and sowed it in grass. At the first cutting the crop was sold for $1,570, leaving a clear profit the first year, over all expenses, of $548.70, and the second year they cleared $975. This was on land that before draining, produced absolutely nothing.

But a drain can be made in a much cheaper manner than by tiles. Should there be plenty of surface rock near, lay one on the bottom of the ditch, one on each side of the bottom rock, and cover with a fourth. Or, instead of using four rocks, a very good ditch can be made by tilting two flat rocks to each other so that a transverse section will form a Λ shaped tunnel, and if there is a firm bed to the ditch it will last an indefinite length of time, the water carrying off the loose crumbs of clay.

Still another plan is to use, instead of the rocks, poles of any kind of wood, so they are straight. Lay two poles, say four or five inches in diameter, parallel to each other, leaving a space of six inches between them, and then lay another pole on the centre space so that the edges will rest on the other two, leaving an open space five or six inches in diameter. Then throw stubble, straw, weeds, leaves or cornstalks over the poles, and indeed over the rocks also, and there will be a good ditch without the outlay of any money. Of course the loose dirt will be thrown over either the rocks or logs. Timber under ground in this way will last a long time.

But there is still another plan, in case the soil has any descent, and there are few lands in Tennessee without it, and that is by means of a subsoil plow. Let a stout subsoil plow follow in the furrow of a turning plow, both drawn by stout teams, and send the subsoiler at least two feet deep. Let the furrows run up and down the hill so as to give a regular descent to the water, and the hard pan broken up by the subsoil will carry off all superfluous water after rains in a very short time. This process is so effective that it is pursued in some sections to the exclusion, entirely, of regular draining. It will have to be repeated at intervals of three or four years, and there will be but little disturbance to the sod, as the subsoiler has only an iron bar for a helve, which raises the surface so slightly it can easily be pressed back with a roller.

From all the testimony to be gathered on this subject, it is pretty apparent that the cost of draining a meadow will be paid the first year by the increased production of the crop. The after-crops will be profits to the farmer.

After what has been said in regard to almost every kind of grass, it is almost needless to impress on the mind of the farmer the necessity of thoroughly pulverizing the soil. Let it be well and deeply broken up, and then with the harrow, drag and roller continue to work it until it is smooth and not a clod appears on the surface. The roots of grasses are exceedingly delicate and cannot penetrate the hard, dry lumps of soil, but will exhaust their energies in going around or under them. Besides, in exactly the same proportion as the clods exist, are the nourishing elements locked up from the use of the grass. Another reason : When clods exist in great numbers, the ground will be rough and the seed will not get into the soil, or will get in too deep to germinate. Thus seeds are lost and the stand impaired.

It is needless to say the soil must be fertile, for nothing will thrive well on poor soil. If it is not rich it must be made so. Should it be desired to sow a field that has been greatly exhausted, a plan pursued in England is commended. The fall previous to

sowing, the field is put in turnips. During the winter, by means of hurdles, a flock of sheep is confined to a portion of the field, and they are not allowed to leave until every vestige of the turnips is exhausted. By this time the ground will be black with their droppings. In this manner the whole field, acre by acre, is gone over, and the ground has a fine covering of manure. We will suppose this consumes the winter. In the spring break up, or to break up just as soon as the sheep are removed is better, and sow with peas. When this crop is in full bearing let on both hogs and sheep, and it will amply repay all its preparation by the manner in which the stock will thrive, and they will again bestow on it a covering of fine manure. Now the ground is well manured and fully capable of giving, in return for the care bestowed, a bountiful crop the first
• year. Of course it must be again broken and pulverized as before mentioned. This not only pays better than letting it lie in fallow, but it keeps down weeds. When ground is fallowed, there will be generally an interval of neglect, and the weeds, ever watchful for a chance, will spring up, mature their seeds and sow them, to the trouble and vexation of the farmer afterward.

SELECTION OF SUITABLE SEEDS AND BEST METHOD OF MIXING THEM.

Whatever the character of the soil to be converted into a meadow, a suitable grass will be found in our list. There are grasses for rocky land, sandy land, bottom land, upland, or calcareous land, and we cannot do better than to refer the reader to the large list from which to select, as the kind of land to which they are adapted is clearly shown in each descriptive article.

It is well known to every farmer that some grasses will not thrive on certain characters of soil. What grasses to sow must be left to the judgment of the farmer, as only an extended experience will be able to show under every circumstance the peculiarities of the land to be sown. Under certain conditions, too, it may be preferable to put the land down in clover, whatever kind of soil it may be; especially is this the case where the land, from long cultivation, is not in good heart. It must be remembered that, if a field has, by long continued cultivation, without rotation, been so reduced in fertility that it will not produce remunerative crops, it will not produce any kind of grass in paying quantities, until some of its vitality has been restored. If a farmer fattens stock from the produce of his own farm, it follows that whatever goes to produce bone, muscle and blood, is so much substance taken from the soil, and restitution is demanded.

When the earth is covered with grasses, and they are plowed under, and converted into vegetable mould, not only does the land receive what has been taken from it, but there is added a vast amount of substances extracted from the atmosphere, such as carbon, ammonia, nitrogen and oxygen, and in that way the land is constantly improved. It is in this way that nature renews herself, and a piece of land left to her care, will, after the lapse of a few years, regain its fertility. But the necessities of man are such he cannot await this slow process, and therefore, it is that he must, to bring about the same result sooner, resort to the expedient of plowing in green crops. Various kinds of green manuring crops are used for this purpose. In the selection of a crop to plow under, one thing should be kept prominently in view, and that is, select such crops as derive their nourishment in great part from the air. It has been demonstrated by many experiments that the legumins do this more effectually than any other class. Among these none are so effectual as the different kinds of clover. They not only enrich the land by the great mass of foliage and stems, but also, by their mechanical displacement of the soil, loosen and pulverize it. Next to the clovers are peas. They, it is true, do not have the same extensive system of roots, but, if possible, they grow and exist more from atmospheric influences than any other plant.

After the selection of the kinds of grass to be sown, the next consideration is to select good seed. How often has it occurred to every farmer to see the result of all his toil and expense culminate in failure for want of good seed! It does not always occur to the sower that his seeds are defective through age, or through mixing noxious seeds with the grass seeds. The high price that seeds command is a great temptation to the dishonest dealer. Sometimes it happens that good seeds are kept until they have lost their power of germinating. It is better to save seed from the farm if possible. It involves but little care to do so, and is an actual saving to the farmer, and then he knows what he is sowing. Should it be necessary, however, to buy seeds, always delay a few days to test them. This is easily done by placing a certain ascertained number on a wet cloth folded several times to retain moisture, and covering them over with a single thickness of the same. Keep the cloth damp a few days and the good ones will swell up and sprout, while the defective ones will be covered over with mould. Count the sprouts, and, by an easy computation, one can then ascertain the proportion of good seeds. Then sow in the proportion and there will be no difficulty in securing a stand. The wisdom of this precaution may be known when it is stated that nearly all the grass seeds are worthless at the end of three years, only a small proportion of them germinating. Even clover seeds, that will keep their vitality when in the ground and covered up, will lose this vitality in four or five years, if exposed to the atmosphere. The millets are scarcely worth sowing after the second year.

No pasture, however luxuriant, is found to consist of one grass alone. In all meadows sown alone, there will be found naked spots, and these seem to depend upon some incompatibility of the soil, at that point, with the grass sown. These spots would be occupied possibly by other species if sown, and thus the whole surface would be covered. Some grasses are disposed to turf the ground, while others form tussocks, therefore it is best to mix, if sowing a tussock grass, a grass that will turf well. Some grasses have a heavy undergrowth of surface foliage, while others have this sparingly. These two peculiarities would be done away with if the two were combined.

It is not, however, proper to combine the pasture grasses with the meadow grasses. As a rule the former have creeping roots and are more vigorous than the latter, and they would soon overpower them and destroy the meadow. This, of course, is spoken in reference to the perennial pasture grasses.

Another condition of mixing the number to be combined. As a rule, it is beyond question that a meadow sown with a variety of seeds will do better and make more hay than when one kind is used. It is no easy matter to explain why, but nature does it, and she rarely errs in her primitive growth.

A custom prevails among the grass farmers of the North and East to mix a great number together—some having as many as a dozen different kinds on one meadow. In this way those vacant spots we have spoken of will be filled up with selected seeds instead of seeds of an inferior or noxious sort. The ground will be covered, and it is better to select the best varieties. The more especially is this the case when it is expected, as most farmers will do, to pasture to some extent the meadow, or when it is wished to train it as a meadow a few years and ultimately let it pass into a grazing lot. It is quite a common custom in this State to mix clover and orchard grass, or clover and Herd's grass, or clover and timothy, and sometimes timothy and Herd's grass are mixed, and this is about the extent of mixing done.

In the great meadows of the Northwestern and New England States where grass culture has been practiced for years, it has been demonstrated often that the admixture of several varieties increases many fold the yield of grass, even if not wanted for pasturage. It secures an early stand, and if the ground fails to suit one species, another will flourish, and thus all vacant spots are covered. These spots of even an inch or two may seem insignificant, but when they are multiplied all over a large field they will materially affect the yield. The crop is made up of single stalks, and every stem is of importance in the aggregation.

It should be kept in mind in the selection of seeds to put those together that will blossom at the same time, unless it is intended for a pasture, in which case the reverse should be considered, for then it is best to so arrange it as to have a succession of ripening crops, and the stock can be supplied throughout the year with such grasses as will be young, tender and succulent.

Some require or are improved by the tramping of stock. If left to themselves they have a tendency to tuft or spring out of the soil until their roots are exposed, when they fall a prey to the sun or to the freezes. These tufts or tussocks, as they are also called, will leave at least half the ground bare, and thus, also, much of the hay is lost. But if tramped by stock, the grass is pressed back into the soil and a turf is kept up that covers the whole surface.

Some of the grasses, however, as timothy, do not require and will not bear grazing for various reasons. These grasses ought not to be mixed with those that are benefitted by timothy, and should such be disposed to tuft, the use of a heavy roller is the only remedy and the vacant spaces can easily be reset by sowing seeds of the same or other varieties on them, and then giving them a light coat of manure.

It may be assumed that in nearly all meadows or pastures clover should be a constituent. It is an easy matter to secure a stand of

6

it. The clover will, in the course of two or three years, disappear from the meadow, leaving the grass in possession of the ground. But it has not left without a blessing, for it has reached up into the air with its long arms and drawn down great stores of ammonia, nitrogen, carbonic acid and other valuable elements that grass requires, and has pushed them down into the soil ; while on the other hand it has pumped up immense quantities of potash and other salts that are, in their natural state, insoluble, and not available to the grasses, and when it dies it bequeaths these valuable manures to its successors. Nor is this all. Its long roots permeat the ground to a prodigious depth for so humble a plant, and when the roots decay the soil is so honey-comed that rains penetrate to the subsoil easily, and the grass roots follow to a much greater depth than they could otherwise attain. And while all these services are being rendered, the clover is giving to its owner large yields of the best of hay.

Such a mixture should be made in the sowings as if one species failed another will take hold. Nor is it proper to sow the same quantities on the different soils of the State. On rich bottoms there will be a necessity for using a free hand, while on the sandy uplands we must withhold the quantity. It may be wished to pasture alternate years, or after the lapse of a few years altogether. All these reasons will modify the quantity of seed to be sown. If a very early crop is wanted, such should be selected as come in early, or if a succession of crops be desired, it will be an easy matter to take from our list those that will ripen, or rather blossom one after another to the latest, thus enabling the farmer to save all his hay in good time. This custom prevails to some extent in Ireland, to sow the same quantity of seed to an acre of each kind as though no other sorts were to be sown, and enough of each kind to fully seed the land.

On a visit to the Unaka Mountains, last September, in company with some members of the Association for the Advancement of Science, we saw some grasses growing in great luxuriance on the "Balds" of that range, and on the top of the Roan Mountain that we had never seen elsewhere, but Prof. Chickering, of Washington City, recognized them as similar to those seen on Mt. Washington and in Canada. There were *poa annua*, the spear grass of Maine, but common on low lands in the State ; *agrostis perennans*, or thin grass, a plant peculiar to marshy places; *phleum alpinum*, *carex juncea*, a rush looking sedge, or rather a grass-like sedge ; *aira flexuosa*, or wood hair grass, an ornamental grass of the Northern latitudes ; *danthonia compressa*, or wild oat grass, and *trisetum molle*, or downy persoon. Besides these were many others not determined by any of the botanists in the company. These grasses afford an immense pasturage during the summer to vast herds of cattle that are driven by the citizens for miles around to summer on them. Gen. Wilder, who owns a large section of land there, informed us the grass, when enclosed from the stock, grew to the height of four feet. Very many varieties existed, all growing promiscuously together. This goes far to show the great difference of the development of the species in different localities, for at lower altitudes, with the exception of the *carex juncea*, these grasses grow quite low.

TIMES AND MANNER OF SOWING.

Up to 1810 the almost invariable rule among all farmers was to sow grass seeds in the spring of the year on crops of grain. Since that time the practice has changed to a great extent, and while some still adhere to spring sowing, the great majority of farmers sow in the early fall. Some few sow grass alone, but the most of them sow with some kind of grain. The former is most decidedly the best, and should in every possible case be practiced. There are many who contend it is much better to sow alone, as the half crop that will be harvested the next year is fully equivalent to the value of the grain crop, while if the two are sown together, they both work injuriously on each other. The stand of grass is injured, and the yield of grain is diminished. With all that, the general custom is to sow on grain fields, and wait until the second year for hay. But one thing is very essential, let it be sown with whatever it may, it must be in the ground long enough before frosts to take a deep root, or much of it will be destroyed by cold. Clover must, however, in either case, be reserved until spring, as, when young, it is very sensitive to the effects of cold unless it is sown in August. It is the custom of some farmers to sow clover and other grass seeds mixed, in the last plowing of late corn. Should that course be decided on, the corn must be late, and plowed on the level principle, and the clover sown after the last plowing. Some crops have succeeded admirably put in on this plan. But the better plan will be to prepare the ground well, as already stated, and sow the seed, if alone, from the 15th of September to the 15th of October; if with a grain crop, as soon as it can be put in safely. Wheat is sown, as a general practice, too late to insure a stand of grass that will resist the winter, and it is, therefore, better to sow rye or barley. Let the time of sowing be when it may, the farmer must watch for a season, otherwise the moisture brought up by plowing will be sufficient to germinate the seeds, but not to make them live, and even if the moisture is not enough to make them germinate, there may be enough to sprout them, and they will still be destroyed.

If it is the intention to sow on a stubble, it is better, as soon as possible after harvest, to prepare the land and sow in some of the August seasons, and if sown then, the clover sowing may not be deferred, but sown with the other seeds, as they will have ample time then to root enough to withstand the cold of winter. Timothy or Herd's gras sown in September or October alone, will always make a good crop the next summer.

As compared with spring sowing, we may safely prefer fall. Both heat and cold are injurious to young grass plants, but of the two, cold is much less injurious than the droughts of summer. It was the experience of the writer, on one occasion, to sow a large meadow. He began about the 1st of September and sowed on until rains stopped him, and again in the middle of October, and finished early in March. On the September sowing there was a magnificent stand that stood over the ground with a solid turf. On the October crop the stand was fair, but much was destroyed during the winter, and the weeds were very troublesome the next year. On the March sowing the stand promised as well as the September crop, but the droughts of summer destroyed it completely.

But there will always be a difference of opinion on this subject, and this difference mainly arises from the difference in the character of soils. Some soils are better sown in the spring, while others secure better results by fall sowing—and in either case the successful farmer will advocate his plan. But in either case, as Gen. Harding truthfully says, a man will fail sometimes, let him sow as he will.

A few words are only necessary in regard to the manner of sowing. In the first place, the ground should be thoroughly prepared, and a season on hand, and if rain has fallen since the ground was put in order and packed the surface, run a sharp toothed harrow over it to break up the crust, then sow the seed and roll it in. A light harrowing will also do on clayey soils. If its surface is too rocky, stumpy or sloping, to admit a roller, the next best thing is to brush it with a light full brush. If the surface is perfectly smooth before the seeds are sown a light brushing does very well, but if it is not, a roller is preferable, as it will not cover so deeply as a brush. Remember that all seeds covered two inches deep will not germinate. If sown with grain, smooth the ground over with a brush after the grain is sown, and let a hand follow immediately behind and cast the seed into the brush. Never use a heavy thin brush, but if the limbs are full of twigs it will not matter as to weight. Then it will not cover too deeply.

It may be necessary, and generally is, to roll the land in the spring, especially if the meadow is a stiff clay soil, as the frosts of winter will usually heave up most of the soil, thereby carrying up roots and earth, and unless it is packed in again the succeeding droughts will surely destroy the grass. All these directions are not to be taken as applying to every locality, or situation, for as difference of soil and climate affects the results, so only can experience, controlled by reason, govern the complete details of this, or any other species of planting.

CUTTING, CURING AND STORING HAY.

There has been, and still is more differences of opinion among hay farmers, as to the proper time of cutting, than upon any other point connected with hay. There are different times for the different varieties, but as a rule there should be but one way. The time of flowering is, unquestionably, the general indication for the harvest to begin. At this time the saccharine juices that go to the formation and development of the seed, are stored in the stalk and leaves, and if saved then, they will lose only their watery constituents, and the grass will be as palatable and succulent as when standing, and will be eaten clean by all kinds of stock.

Still, some wait until the pollen falls and the seeds are in the milk, and those practicing this plan contend that the hay will not scour the horses so badly. But there is another reason why some defer the cutting to so late a date, and that is, it will not lose so much water, and consequently will be heavier and so bring more money.

A good authority says: "I cut in the blossom when the hay is designed for milch cows, or for fattening beeves, because in that state it makes more beef, and induces the cows to give more milk ; but if for work stock, horses or oxen, I cut six days later, or thereabouts, because it does not scour or loosen the animal so much as when cut in the blossom." In either case, however, in an extensive crop, if the harvesting begins at the blossoming period, it will be six days before it is finished.

The gama grass and possibly the lucerne should be cut as often as it is high enough to run the mower through them, as they become very hard, stiff and woody if they grow too rank, whereas, they are, if cut in time, very sweet and nutritious.

There is also much difference of opinion in regard to the proper time for cutting clover. Some will take a stalk and tie a knot in it, and if much sap exudes from it, they will leave it until it will barely show moisture. Others will cut when the field is about half in blossom, while still others will defer it until about half the heads are brown and the seed are in a milky state. But the mass of testimony is in favor of cutting clover when a few brown heads show themselves over the field.

It is a well known fact that just before the formation of the seed there is a large per cent of sugar, starch and gluten in the stalk than at any other time. When the grass first springs up it is filled almost entirely with water, as any one can satisfy himself by chewing a stem in its different periods of growth. As the plant grows and matures, the water gradually becomes impregnated with these substances, and at its blossoming period these elements exist in their greatest quantity—in fact, nature is now storing up material from which to form the seed, and these stores are held ready in the stalk, to effect that purpose. These elements are all soluble in water, and consequently, are easily dissolved by the juices of the stomach. But if these principles are allowed to go to seed, they leave the stalk, and at once the plant starts on its downward course, becoming more and more woody, until finally decay sets in, and the hay is then worthless ; because the woody fibre is insoluble in the stomach.

Prof. Kirkland draws the following conclusions from many careful observations as regards timothy :

1. "That timothy is a perennial plant, which renews itself **by**
an annual formation of bulbs," or perhaps, more correctly speaking, tubers, in which the vitality of the plant is concentrated during the winter. These form in whatever locality the plant is
selected, without reference to dryness or moisture. From these
proceed the stalks that support the heads and leaves, and from the
same source spread out the numerous fibres forming the true roots.

2. "To insure a perfect development of tubers a certain amount
of nutrition must be assimilated in the leaves and returned to the
base of the plant, through the stalk.

3. "As soon as the process of nutrition is completed, it becomes
manifest by a state of desiccation or dryness, always commencing
at a point directly above either the first or second joint of the stem
near the crown of the tubers. From this point the desiccation
gradually progresses upward, and the last portion of the stalk
yielding its freshness is that adjoining the head. Coincident with
the beginning of this process, is the full development of the seeds,
and with its progress they mature. Its earliest appearance is evidence that both the tubers and seeds have received their requisite
supplies of nutrition, and that neither the stalk nor the leaves are
longer necessary to aid them in completing their maturity. A
similar process occurs in the onion just above the bulb, indicating
a maturity of that organ.

4. "If the stalk be cut from the tubers before this evidence of
maturity appears, the necessary supplies of nutrition will be arrested, their proper growth will cease, and an effort will be made
to repair the injury by sending out small lateral tubers, from which
weak, unhealthy stalks will proceed at the expense of **the** original
tubers. All will ultimately perish, either by the drought of autumn
or the cold of winter.

5. "The tubers, together with one or two of the lower joints of
the stalk, remain fresh and green during the winter, if left to take
their natural course; but if, by any means, this green portion be
severed, at any season of the year, the result is the death of the
plant."

From these five propositions the following conclusions are
drawn:

1. "The timothy grass cannot, under any circumstances, be
adapted for pasture, as the close nipping of horses and sheep is

fatal to the tubers, which are also extensively destroyed by swine, if allowed to run in the pasture.

2. "That the proper time for mowing timothy is at any time after the process of desiccation has commenced on the stalk, as noted in the third proposition. It is not very essential whether it is performed a week earlier or later, provided it be postponed till that evidence of maturity has become manifested.

3. "All attempts at close shaving the sward should be avoided while using the scythe, and in gauging the mowing machines, care should be taken to run them so high that they will not cut the timothy below the second joint above the tuber."

CUTTING.

Perhaps no invention of agricultural machinery—and their name is legion—has afforded more positive benefit to the farmer than the introduction of the mowing machine. Before its invention no farmer could, with certainty and success, secure a large amount of hay. It ripens in the hottest of the weather, and at a time when the labor of the country is, as a general thing, all actively employed; so if a man did get enough, it was at an exhorbitant price, fearfully reducing his profits. Then the grass, if of one crop, all needs cutting at once, so it would be impracticable to save it all in prime condition.

Another improvement is the horse rake. The first one used was the horizontal rake, that running under the swath heaped it up until the teeth were full, when by a slight lift of the handles it turned over, leaving the hay in windrows. This it did very well, and still does well, but another has come into very general use that is a little more extensive, but gives the driver a seat on it, and certainly gathers up the grass cleaner than the other.

The Tedder is another machine that is used extensively in the Northern States, where the weather is more uncertain than here, and the hay dries much slower than beneath the Southern sun. It is seldom used in Tennessee, and is but seldom necessary.

CURING.

This is a point upon which there is as much difference of opinion, perhaps, as on any other point connected with harvesting. Some prefer to let it get dry on the ground, just as it is left by the mower while others cure it in the windrow, and still others cure it in the

cock. This refers to the true grasses, for almost every one **who**
makes hay of the clover pursues one plan, which will be spoken of
directly. This difference in the plans of curing results chiefly from
the great difference there is in the curing quality of the various
grasses. Timothy cures much easier and quicker than Herd's
grass, while the coarser grasses, such as Gama, Egyptian and others,
require still longer time than Herd's grass. Formerly, it was the
universal custom to allow it to lie until it was almost dry before
raking, but that custom is fast giving place to a more rapid method.
Now, with many of our best farmers, it is deemed **sufficient to**
allow it to remain on the ground after cutting a time only long
enough for it to become wilted, and then with a rake it is put into
windrows. Hands follow immediately with hand rakes or pitch-
forks, and throw it up into cocks. Some do not even cock it, but,
if the weather is favorable, allow it to remain in the windrow for a
day, or the second evening after cutting, and then gather it up in
wagons and carry to the rick or barn. But probably the surest
plan is to put it into cocks the evening after it is cut in the morning, and allow it to remain in this state for two or three days, according as the promise of good weather may be, then throw open
the cocks and spread the hay, before hauling up. It can be easily
determined at this stage whether or not it is sufficiently cured. If,
when examined, the cocks have become heated, by opening them
out the heat that has been generated will readily become dissipated,
and there is not much likelihood of its becoming again heated.
One fact is well ascertained, and that is, the sooner it goes into the
rick or barn after cutting, without spoiling, the better will be the
hay, and the more will it be relished by stock.

Some farmers adopt the plan of arresting its disposition to heat
by sprinkling salt upon it as it is stored. This is a good plan, and
increases the fondness of stock for it if too much is not applied.
One hand should apply the salt as it is thrown in, at the rate of
about two quarts to the two-horse wagon load.

Should the farmer not wish to sell his hay, and is scarce of a supply, he can increase the quantity of provender by mixing, as it is
put into the heap, a third or even a half of straw, or inferior hay,
that has been left over, and in the curing process which takes place
the juices of the new hay will penetrate and sweeten the straw,

greatly improving its character, without deteriorating its own quality.

A most excellent farmer says he waits until the dew is off, then starts his mower, and in the evening about four o'clock starts the rake, and has hands following with forks, and by the time the dew is falling has it all in cocks. The next morning, after the dews dry up, he opens and throws out the cocks, and immediately after dinner begins to haul to the barn.

When it is intended to let it remain in the cocks for several days, great care should be exercised in properly forming the hay into cocks in view of wet weather. Cocks indifferently made would be, if possible, worse than if spread out, for the water would penetrate them all through, and the hay would in a short time mould or rot. In the first place, they should be made large, not less than one hundred pounds in each at any time. Then make them as sharp at the top as possible, so as to be stout and secure against winds. Make the sides nearly perpendicular, and lastly, comb them down well from top to bottom with a pitchfork, so as to throw as many stems as possible parrallel with one another, thatching it well in order the better to shed the water. But even with the most careful management all the outer layer and some of the interior will be destroyed by long continued rains.

Cut clover when the dew is off, let it wilt, and rake it into windrows. Allow it to remain in this state until the dew is off the next morning, and begin at once to haul and place in the barn, sprinkling salt in small quantities over every layer. In this way the entire crop will be exposed only about twenty-four hours, which is amply sufficient for it. It will heat and go through a heavy sweat, but this will not injure it, and it will look as fresh and almost as green when cured as when standing. The salt is essential to its proper preservation.

Should the farmer have a quantity of good clean wheat, oat, or rye straw, it is a very good practice, and a safe one, to throw a layer of it between each load of clover. It will permit the passage of the air, and the aroma of the clover will penetrate the straw, each in this manner benefitting the other, so that both will be eaten with a relish by cattle.

TROUBLESOME PLANTS TO MEADOWS.

There are several plants exceedingly troublesome to the meadows in Tennessee. Among them is the white top (*Erigeron Philadephi-cum*) or fleabane. This is a perennial, and sometimes infests meadows to such an extent as to render them worthless. Meadows troubled with them should be mown several years in succession when the white top begins to blossom. Broom grass (*Andropogon scoparius*) is also very pestiferous, destroying meadows after four or five years unless closely watched, and the **broom** grass cut up by the roots every spring. The trumpet creeper (*Bignonia radicans*) infests meadows in rich bottom lands, and when cut off by the mower forms hard knots, which will arrest the action of the sickle. This vine should be dug up "root and branch." White clover and blue-grass **are** both great enemies to the meadow, and when they prevail to any extent it is best to use the meadow as a pasture, and **sow** another meadow somewhere else.

A top dressing of superphosphate or of stable manure **every fall,** after a crop of hay is taken off, will also do much to keep down noxious weeds and grasses. The farmer should always bear in mind that meadows require to be regularly fed. It is too much to expect that they will grow heavy crops of hay year after year without exhausting the elements in the soil which go to make hay. These elements must be supplied. Restitution must be made if the farmer expects to **have luxuriant** and profitable meadows. The best rule to adopt is, **never to take off a** crop of hay without making a liberal application of manure.

A WORD ABOUT MANURES.

The people of the South have much to learn in regard to the **success-**ful management of meadow lands. Many farmers seem to think it possible to take large crops of hay from the same land year after year without adding any fertilizers. This is a grand mistake. One had just as well expect to check on his bank account day after day without making additions to his deposits, as to check on the soil for large crops without properly feeding the land which grows them.

The question we ought to consider is, how to manage meadows after they are properly sown and a stand of grass secured, so as not only to keep up their fertility, but to increase their power of production.

This question is so well understood by English farmers that they **seldom** take a crop of hay from a piece of land without making a large and expensive application of manure. If the hay is cut several times a year it is a heavy draft upon the soil, and some restitution must be made to the soil or it will soon cease to meet the expectations of the husbandman. The English farmer, enlightened by experience, in order to strengthen the land and stimulate the grass roots to renewed exertion, will draw out upon the meadow various kinds of manure to supply whatever wants he may deem the land requires.

There are not many kinds of manure in reach of a Tennessee farmer, unless he takes the forethought to provide them. But if he does take this in mind, and watches closely for everything that will contribute to this end, he will be surprised himself at the result in a very short time. Besides those elements that are at the command of every careful farmer, there is another class of manures called "artificial," and these can be procured at any place by a sufficient outlay. But they are costly, and it requires a scientific acquaintance with their properties before the ordinary farmer will have the courage to invest in them. In other words, he must be able to see why and how his money will be returned with interest.

In order to properly understand the requirements of plants, it is essential the action of the different manures should be known, together with an approximate knowledge of the constituents of the soil. Soils are the result of the degredation, or breaking down, from various causes, of rocks. Through the great convulsions of nature this triturated dust is mingled together, so that every species of rock formation is represented in every handful of clay. Were this not the case, we would have over limestone rocks a great mass of unproductive pulverized carbonate of lime; or over granite, we would see nothing but the sparkling atoms of quartz and mica, and over each stratum there would be the constituents of that rock, and hence no vegetation would charm the eye or delight the heart, to say nothing of our digestive wants. Through the agency of perfectly natural causes (water principally), the soils have been intimately mingled. By this wise provision vegetation in every spot in the world finds some elements necessary to its existence. But it sometimes happens that there is a deficiency of some of the elements, and again that there is a surplus. In the great alluvial swamps decayed vegetable matters exist to such an extent that some cereals do not thrive well, and on the other hand, on the steep mountain sides, by the action of washing rains, this matter has been carried off. Again, in many sections, the fertile matters have been exhausted, or so nearly so, that the products of the soil cease to be remunerative. It is the province of scientific agriculture to point out these deficiencies and direct the remedy.

The soil originally consisted simply of the debris of the rocks or clay. It is composed of the elements of the rocks, together with an intimate admixture of some mineral substances. In limited patches the soil partakes of the character of the formations underneath. Thus, in iron districts, the soil in places shows the presence, in considerable quantities of iron, making the earth red or brown. In sandstone countries the clay has a quantity of sand overlying it, and among the primitive rocks scales of mica glisten on every side. The weight of a cubic foot of thoroughly dried soil averages as follows :

	Pounds.
Siliceous sand	111.3
Calcareous sand	113.6
Sandy clay	97.8
Loamy clay	88.8
Stiff clay	80.3
Slaty marl	112.
Fertile mould	68.7
Common arable soil	84.5

Chemists, from the earliest times, have been struck with the great proportion of insoluble to soluble substances in the soil. These insoluble substances will resist the action of acid and alkali in any quantities short of destroying vegetation. Analysis have striven by the aid of weak solutions of acids and alkalies to effect this, and though the science is by no means perfect, they have succeeded in rendering much inert matter, that has hitherto cumbered the land into plant food. In an average of many kinds of soil the proportions are, of

Insoluble matters	89.305
Soluble matters	2.047
Phosphate, carbon, and sulphate lime	3.160

Thus it is seen that of the great mass of soil, ranging from a few inches to many hundred feet thick, only a very small per cent is available to vegetation. Further, chemical analysis has also developed the fact that all animal tissues are composed of these identical elements of the soil. Truly and literally we are made of dust; but the animal kingdom does not derive its sustenance directly from the soil—that would be impossible. Our digestive organs are not constructed for that purpose, and could not assimilate such food, though in the great famine of Germany, in the 18th century, the starving millions did essay it only to die in torture. Nature has provided an intermediate agent, vegetation, whose organs are nicely adapted to this purpose. They send down into the soil their sensitive feelers, and pick up such stray bits of food as men or beasts require. They store it away in their granaries until it is called for, and these kind friends are thus the purveyors to animal life. Not only is a man thus directly fed by these natural agents, but, to keep up a constant unceasing supply, a large proportion is sent back to the soil in a form to invigorate man's food. This refunded capital is variously called humin, ulmin, geine. Ulmin, or ulmic acid, is the first formed; humin is formed from ulmin by the absorption of oxygen; geine, or geic acid, from humin by the further absorption of oxygen.

We will describe all these changes, however, under the general term of geine. Under some form geine is essential to agriculture. It is the result of decaying vegetable matter, or, in other words, it is the active principle of mould, and is the direct result of putrefaction. It is carbon, oxygen, and hydrogen. It has a powerful affinity for nitrogen, one of the constituents of the atmosphere, and whenever it comes in contact, the hydrogen of the geine unites with the nitrogen of the air, and ammonia is the result. It also absorbs water freely, and this is why bottom lands, full of geine, fail to suffer from drought. The geine attracts moisture from the air, and keeps the plant alive. These salts, humin, ulmin, and geine, were formerly called extract of mould. They are, for the most part, soluble in water. For the sake of brevity, we will embrace all these salts, as well as crenic and apocrenic acids, convertible with the salts, under the general term *mould*. So far as nourishment is derived from the soil, this substance is the food of plants. It has been deposited over the clay by the general decay of vegetation, through many ages, and according to the amount deposited depends the value of the land.

Why it is that plants live and grow, or how they grow is a mystery no philosopher has ever been able to explain. God gives

the vital principle, and so long as that continues the plant is able
to resist an opposing power, which is chemistry. When life ceases,
chemistry then asserts its power, and decay begins, which leads to
fermentation, and after this process is ended, putrefaction takes
charge, which soon resolves the body into its original elements;
and they are then ready to aid in the construction of another living
body. Thus nothing is ever lost. It may change its location;
the plant that grew at the head of a mountain torrent may ultimately enter into the composition of a sugar cane in the delta of
the Mississippi, but it is still in the universe, silently performing
its duties.

Many things contain salts available to the agriculturist. Lime,
ashes, plaster of Paris (sulphate of lime), saltpetre, common salt,
phosphate of lime, bone dust, coal ashes, hair, hoofs, horns, copperas, and many others. Some of these substances have to be used
sparingly, such as salt or copperas, but all are beneficial to growing
plants.

These substances act chemically, and free a great many inert
matters. Growing plants absorb vast quantities of carbonic acid
through their leaves, and carrying it down, throw it into the soil,
where it acts upon silica and allumina, freeing salts for their
growth.

Wood and coal ashes are very rich in the salts, and furnish one
of the cheapest and best additions that can be made to land. Coal
ashes are not so rich in the various salts, but contain enough to
merit a better fate than is generally awarded them. The composition of wood ashes is as follows:

Two hundred parts of wood ashes contain

	Per cent.
Carbonic acid	58.53
Sulphuric acid	6.43
Phosphoric acid	3.40
Muriatic acid	1.82
Lime	50.35
Magnesia	4.55
Potash and soda	67.96
Silex	5.22
Oxide iron	.50
Oxide manganese	1.10
Water	.14
	200.00

Of this 27.14 parts are soluble at once in water, and leached ashes are deprived of it, and the balance, 172.86 parts, are insoluble, but act slowly on the soil, freeing various substances in the process of time. Coal ashes contain these same ingredients in a much less degree, or if soil is entirely deprived of its vegetable mould, it is identical almost with coal ashes. Each hundred pounds contain eight that are at once valuable to the farmer, and another portion has a prospective value. Coal ashes are worth a good deal simply as a mechanical loosener of the soil. Mixed with it, in even small proportions, it renders the soil friable and easily worked.

Having now explained that there is a principle called mould or geine, and that this principle is necessary to fertility, and, also, that this principle, to be in an available form, must be reacted on by salts, it remains to enquire what is the best form in which these elements are united. Practically, every farmer in the country will at once answer stable manure. And, as is generally the case, practice has long found out what science seeks a reason for. A careful analysis of cow manure, which is generally accepted as the unit of value, shows that cow dung consists, not to go into an ultimate analysis, of

	Per cent.
Water	83.60
Salts	0.95
Geine	15.45

This seems to be a small proportion of valuable matter, only one-sixth of the whole amount. But let us see what a careful farmer can do by saving for a year. In an experiment, conducted carefully and published a few years ago, an average cow was selected, and everything she ate or drank was carefully weighed, as well as all the voidings of dung. This experiment lasted seven days, and from a calculation, this cow would have made in one year, 4,800 pounds geine, 71 pounds bone dust, 37 pounds plaster, 37 pounds lime, 25 pounds common salt, 15 pounds sulphate potash. This, carefully saved, furnishes salts of lime equal to four and a half bushels of corn daily, or 1,662½ annually. Not only is this amount saved, but in addition the nitrogen that is in it, by chemical affinity, creates a large amount of ammonia, that is fixed and amounts in a year to 677 pounds. To the nitrogen is due much of the excellence of this stimulant, and without the animal matter, or nitrogen, it would be nothing more than decayed wood and salts. It is a common idea that the activity of stable manure is due entirely to the animal excrements. It is due rather to the happy combination of ammonia, geine, and salts, such as no chemist can manufacture from the food of the cow. Were this possible, a pile of rotted hay and turnips would supply all these united elements. But effort has demonstrated that it cannot be done. Nor does the food of a cow affect, but little, the elements of dung. A cow fed on rich nitrogenous food, such as corn or oats, will give some more nitrogen in the dung, and form more ammonia, but the salts and geine will be but little changed.

Horse dung is much richer in manures than cow dung; but horse dung very quickly ferments, and, by fermentation, it will lose one-third its value in one month. It is, therefore, very necessary to remove, as often as possible, the horse dung from the stable, and place it in the compost heap with the cattle dung, or with alternate layers of soil, and sprinkled with lime or plaster. These salts will catch and fix the escaping ammonia, and prevent much loss. After horse dung has fermented, if alone, it is of far less value than cow dung, but before it ferments it is much more valuable. When that process is completed fully, nine-tents of its value, according to our best writers, is lost. These are statements based, not only on experience and observation, but also on absolute chemical analyses. How much it stands the farmer in hand then to observe a systematic saving and storing of these treasures of agricultural wealth! A compost heap, under a good shelter, is to the uninformed a heap reeking with filth, repulsive to the eye and offensive to the olfactories. But to the scientific farmer it is a bed of power. In it are contained the yellow grain and the luscious fruit; over it hovers the spirit of the rose and the lily, and sweet odors are stored in it, to make the fragrant pink and the delicious heliotrope. Let every consideration of economy and enterprise stimulate the farmer, then, to save every waste of the farm. The Chinese are so sensible of the importance of manure, in a country teeming with an over population, where the soil is tasked to its utmost to carry its population, they even save the parings of their finger and toe nails to add to its fertility. The farmer has a wonderful bank to draw upon for this purpose. Cattle and horse dung and urine, the scrapings of

7

the barnyard after every rain, straw, stalks, leaves of the forest, drifts on the banks of streams, all contribute their share in the general enrichment of the farm. And any one would be surprised at the amount accumulated for the spring scattering, if systematically carried on for one year. It requires but a little time, too, if a regular time be given to it. Regularlity and system are the great watchwords of improvement.

Millions of dollars are annually wasted by burning straw and stalks, which, if carried to the stables and barn yard, would act as solvents, to catch this daily waste. If the ashes, resulting from the burning straw, were as good manure as the straw itself, then burning would not be wasteful. But a large amount of valuable matter goes into the air as gases, besides much is blown away by the winds. A Mr. Lawes, of England, determined this matter of burning manure in an experiment that was both fair and positive. He took 28 tons of yard manure, and divided it; fourteen tons were reduced by fire, leaving 32 cwt. of ashes. He then scattered the fourteen tons of manure left ou one acre of land, and the 32 cwt. of ashes on another acre of land, and left another acre without any application. He cultivated them all well and alike.

The manured acre made twenty-two bushels of wheat, the ashed acre made sixteen bushels, and the unmanured acre made sixteen bushels. This proves that the more nitrogen manure contains in combination with the salts, the more value it has.

Night soil, or the excrement of human beings, is, next to chicken manure, the richest and most stimulating of all manures. Then comes that of fattening hogs and sheep, horses and cows. But, as before stated, the disposition to waste is so great, that the "cold" manures, as that of cows, sheep and hogs, are more available to the farmer than the more active ones of man and horse.

Too much care cannot be exercised in preserving the excrements of men and animals. Every pound of ammonia that is lost or evaporates represents the amount required for a bushel of corn ; and every pound of the urine of a horse or man will furnish sufficient ammonia for a pound of wheat ; and two and a half pounds of the urine of man will furnish the phosphoric acid and more than half of the potash required for a pound of wheat.

It then remains for us to make the application of these remarks, and every right-thinking man will see at once the importance of gathering up and saving. It is money in his pocket. One man will burn a few bushels of soil, and setting it near the privy, will throw, every day, a few handsfull on the pile of excrement, and in a few months he will fill his barrels with the most valuable pondrette, that another man will go to the city and pay a large price for. One man will set a few barrels of ashes in a convenient place, and cause the house-cleaner to empty the urine of the night into them. In a few months he will have his ashes thoroughly saturated with salts and organic matter the most valuable.

In England, farmers do not consider it any hardship to dig cisterns, in which to save all the liquid excrements of the cows and horses, and with a water cart, spread it over their pastures and meadows.

Many object to the use of human excrement, on account of its offensiveness. This can be easily prevented, and at the same time by an agent that is a valuable addition to the manure heap. The sulphate of iron (copperas), is a powerful deodorizer, and a few cents worth added to the night soil deprive it of any offensive smell for a length of time sufficiently long to remove it.

A great many bones are wasted on every farm that make valuable manure, and are easily prepared for use. Let a barrel be devoted to bones, and whenever a bone is thrown into it, cover it up with unleached ashes. Let the barrel stand in the weather, and in a few months the bones will be so friable they may be easily broken and converted into an unadultered bone dust, better than can be bought in any of the agricultural stores. Or, if he cannot wait this slow process, they are easily burned and crushed.

In making soap, much fine phosphate of lime is thrown out in the shape of half eaten bones, and in spent lie. Soap suds are also a fine addition to the manure or compost heap. In these are found not only the alkalies of soda and potash, but also much nitrogenous matter in the shape of grease. All these assist in enriching our heap.

No farm yard is without the best guano. It is true, the guano of the shops is from sea birds, whose food is fish, but the guano of the chicken house is exceedingly valuable and well worth saving. Mixing it with soil or ashes and sowing over a garden plat, rather thinly, for it is very rich, its effects are seen to the row. However, the dung of fowls and especially of pigeons, is best applied in the form of solution. It is not so apt to burn up the plant in this manner. One part of manure to ten parts of water will make a fine wash for vines, or for fruit trees it is unexcelled. Another addition to the heap is skins, carrion, either of animals or fowls, scales of fishes, hair, hoofs, and in fact, every kind of animal substance that may come within reach that is worthless. Instead of dragging off dead horses or cows, as an attraction for buzzards and dogs, cut them up and let them add to the manure heap. In this way a valuable addition will be made.

Among the richest of all manures, not excepting animal matters even, is soot. It is not only rich in salts, but in geine. It is said there are as much salts in 100 lbs. of soot as there are in one ton of cow dung. Nothing is better for vegetables, than an application of water with soot dissolved in it. Besides, bugs are not fond of it, and it drives them away. Throw all the soot of the chimneys, by all means, on the heap.

Sheep dung is one of our finest manures, and what is better, the animals do the spreading themselves. A worn-out meadow or pasture if given to the sheep, and they are kept in it any length of time, will be restored to its pristine fertility. It is said that 1,000 sheep run on a piece of ground one year will make the soil capable of yielding grain enough, over and above the capacity of the soil without the sheep manure, to support 1,035 sheep an entire year. Unless the sheep are nightly folded, however, the manure cannot be gathered. If it can be collected, put on the pile, by all means.

We have now enumerated the principal sources whence a farmer can draw his supplies without drawing upon his pocket. Many kinds, under our system of farming, are unavailable to the farmer. I mean the liquids. Without floors to the stables and pig-pens, the urine, which is the richest of manures, so far as salts are concerned, is wasted. But he can save his own, and the excrements of one man, properly saved for one year, will well manure one acre of land. Why let these rivers of wealth flow away from the farm? He prefers going to the shops and buying worse than he can prepare on his farm.

There are many artificial manures for sale. Plasters from Kentucky and Virginia; phosphate of lime from South Carolina; bone dust from the large cities, and many other mixtures and compounds.

But scarcely a farmer but what has at his command a manure, rich in every respect and with the addition of a cheap alkali, equal in chemical properties to cow dung: I mean the scrapings of ponds, and the mud of rivers and creeks. West Tennessee has an area containing pure muck, the balance of the State has no such advantage; but next to muck, and nearly as valuable, is pond and river mud. By the addition of two pounds of sal soda or potash, such as is used for washing purposes, to 100 lbs. of muck, the mass becomes, as near as possible cow dung. So here we have an almost inexhaustible supply of cow dung, without its smell or offensiveness. The green sand beds in West Tennessee also will supply fertilizers in unlimited quantities.

Here then, the provident farmer has all that is requisite to enrich his grounds before seeding to grass. It is needless to say that clover, as a preceding crop to land that is about to enter the long and tedious travail of meadow, is absolutely requisite. But after it is started, the farmer need not think, for one moment, that grass adds to its fertility. It does not, but on the other hand detracts just what the farmer cuts off; and if he is a wise farmer, he will put it back in a shape to increase his drafts on it.

When a meadow or pasture becomes packed, from too much pasturage, it will be well enough to run a subsoil through it occasionally. This loosens the under sod, and the narrow helve does not tear up the turf. Of course the land has been, if required, well drained. In addition to this, for the renovation of such lands, the application of manure is indispensable. It should be applied immediately after a cutting, as it will stimulate the roots, made weak by being deprived of their foliage, to renewed growth, and prevent much of it from drying. Of course it must be done by top dressing, and by far the most efficacious plan is to apply it in the liquid form. It may be done by diluting the manure with from five to ten parts of water, and using a cart, such as is used for sprinkling streets. Another, and the most common way, is to drive through the meadow with a load of good compost, such as we have described, and with two hands in the rear of the wagon with shovels, it can be scattered broadcast as fast as the team will walk.

Pastures treated to a top-dressing after every cutting could, like the English pastures, instead of three acres to the ox, feed three oxen to one acre, and the meadows would not yield a scanty ton

to the acre, but we could continue to cut until stopped by cold
weather. An English tenant will pay ten pounds ($50) rent per
acre for meadows, and get always two, frequently three, crops per
year, yielding from three to five tons per acre. We could do this
also by following the same system of farming, and that is to run
the manure wagon constantly.

DHOURO CORN, DURRA OR DOURA, INDIAN MILLET—
(Sorghum vulgare.)

In the West Indies, it is called *guinea corn*, in Arabia, *dhouro*, in
India, *jovaree*, and in China, *nagara*. In some countries it is cultivated as a forage plant, the stems containing a large proportion of
saccharine matter, and when dry affording a fine hay, though rough.
The nutritive quality of the seeds nearly equals that of wheat.
From its resemblance to Indian corn, in the south of Europe, it is
called *small maize*. On rich land it grows from eight to twelve
feet high, and it produces more bushels of seed than any other
known cereal to the acre.

There are several varieties of this cereal, being sports from the
original. Chocolate corn, Tennessee rice, chicken corn, are some
of its synonyms. It is a native of Central Asia, and is cultivated
extensively in Asia, Africa, West Indies, Brazil, and in the southern part of the United States. It will grow to perfection from
Pennsylvania to Florida. There are two varieties usually cultivated, the " white" and the "red," both good, but the red produces a great many more seeds—some say as many as four times
the quantity of the other. The red matures earlier, too ; the white,
being in higher latitudes, is often caught by frosts. The latter,
however, is preferable when intended for food. A failure of this
crop in Arabia and Africa, would be as great a calamity as that of
corn in the United States. The meal is white and makes delicious
breakfast cakes, and is said to be much better than corn meal.

Its yield varies according to the soil on which it is sown. On
rich sandy loam or alluvial bottoms, it will make from 100 to 150
bushels per acre, but unlike the other cereals, except buckwheat, it
will grow well on soil however poor. On rocky clayey land, that
will scarcely sprout foxtail, I have seen the most luxuriant crops.
It will continue to grow until frost, and after the first head matures

it throws out succors from other joints, and makes smaller heads. This is expedited by going over it and culling out as fast as it ripens. Stock of all kinds are fond of it, and will greedily eat it. It is almost equal to Indian corn for fattening food for hogs.

The ground is plowed as well as possible, and then thrown into low ridges, or even better, no ridges at all; the seeds are then drilled three feet apart, with a seed drill. If sown by hand, the rows are made with a bull-tongue plow and covered with a harrow. A peck of seeds is enough for an acre, unless they are weevil eaten, when more should be used. They should be covered very lightly, not more than an inch and a half deep. When they come up they should be thinned out by chopping across the row, leaving the plants eighteen inches apart, then one or two good plowings are all the crop requires. There need be no fear of weeds or grass after it once starts out to grow, as its enormous foliage, and thickly clustering suckers choke out everything else on the ground. It grows very rapidly, and will soon be ready for harvesting. There are various ways for doing this, according to the fancy of the farmer. Some cut off the seed heads as they ripen, and turn stock on the stalks, which will eat them up quite clean. Others will cut the stalks just before frost, scouring them and feeding them as hay through the winter; and these stalks will keep better than any other of the pithy grasses, not securing like Indian corn or sugar cane. Still others wait until the largest quantity of seeds is ripe, and then cut, and house seeds, stalks and all together. If the fodder is pulled it makes excellent feed, in fact every part of the plant makes good feed for some animals. Care should be exercised to protect it from fowls, as they are so fond of the seeds that, frequently, whole fields are stripped.

It is often planted in the missing places of corn, and it does far better than a replant of corn, as one stalk will throw out numerous suckers, making several large heads and ripening with the corn. Drought has but little effect in retarding its growth. It retains its dark green color and luxuriant foliage when other plants are shriveled up by the heat.

In the South it is sown thickly in drills, and cut for soiling stock, and if not allowed to flower, it will bear cutting until frost comes. Many sow it broadcast for hay. Prepare the ground well, and sow one bushel of seed to the acre, harrowing it in. It makes

an enormous yield of hay, but, from the succulent character of the
stalks, it is difficult to cure, unless a good "spell" can be caught.
However, if the farmer has a drove of mules or steers to fatten, he
can cut a load or two at a time, throwing it into a rack, which can
be replenished as required, and the hay will remain green on the
ground until frost, so that there is no danger of its being lost by
becoming too ripe.

In Germany the seeds are deprived of the chaff and used as rice,
and sells for the same price. In Asia and Africa it is made into a
meal and eaten either in gruel, cakes or bread. It can be sown at
any time from the first of April (a light frost not injuring it) until
the first of July.

If fed on the ground the stalks will remain in the way of the
planter for a year at least, but if plowed under in the fall like
broom corn, they will rot by spring, and if lime is sown on them
before plowing under, it will greatly expedite the process, and the
soil will improve every year.

Taking into consideration, the fact that it will yield more seed,
fodder and stalks on a greater variety of soils, with less labor, in
any kind of season, and return more litter to the land than any
other cereal, and being a good food for man and beast, it may be
justly considered one of the most valuable of the cereals. And with
these facts it is most surprising that it is raised to the small extent
it is.

About twenty-five or thirty years ago it could be seen on the
plantation of almost every farmer in the Stats. It gave very general satisfaction, and yet it went out as suddenly as it came into
popularity. This was due to the cry that it impoverished the land.
This verdict was accepted without question, and its culture aban-
doned; but it is manifest, from subsequent experiments, that it
detracts as little from the fertility of the soil as any other cereal—
much less than some.

If the stalks are left and only the grain and fodder removed,
and the farmer fed on the field and plowed in as before stated, the
soil will not be greatly injured. It will not kill cattle like clover,
and no care is necessary but to salt and water them. One would
be surprised how quickly cattle will fatten on the bare stalks, and
besides they will leave the ground covered ankle deep with manured stalks.

With all these facts before us, and our own experience in its cultivation, we most heartily commend its use to the citizens of Tennessee. There is no character of soil, from the rich alluvial bottoms of the Mississippi to the sterile mountain lands of East Tennessee, but will make good crops of dhouro corn, and we would like to see it on every farm.

The following analysis of the green fodder and green clover will show their comparative values :

Red clover in blossom :

Water	78.0
Organic matter	20.3
Ash	1.7
Albuminoids	3.7
Carbohydrate	8.6
Crude fibre	8.0
Fat	0.8

Dhouro :

Water	77.3
Organic matter	21.4
Ash	1.1
Albuminoids	2.9
Carbohydrate	11.9
Crude fibre	6.7
Fat	1.4

It has more heating properties and more fat producing principles than red clover, but is not so rich in flesh formers.

PEA—(*Pisum Sativum.*)

The pea is a native of Southern Europe, and its cultivation extends into every State. The varieties are very great, and while some are cultivated extensively for table use, other kinds are raised for stock and for manurial purposes. Our garden pea was cultivated by the Greeks and Romans. Peas were found in the ancient Swiss lake dwellings. They were introduced into England in the time of Henry VIII., and is there still a standard crop. They are sown or drilled in, and are sometimes even sown with oats, the two being harvested and fed together. Sheep and hogs are very fond of them, and especially are the vines prized as a sheep fodder. Analysis shows that peas contain : ash, 2.5 ; albuminoids or flesh formers, 22.4 ; carbohydrates or heaters, 52.3 ; crude fibre, 9.2 ; fat, 2.5 ; water, 14.3. The composition shows them to be very nutritious, and animals fatten rapidly when fed with them liberally. The pea haulm, when dry, gives, by analysis, water, 14.3 ; ash, 4 ; albuminoids, 6.5 ; carbohydrates, 35.2 ; crude fibre, 40 ; fat, 2. This shows the haulm to be three times as valuable for feeding purposes as wheat straw, and a little more valuable as a feed than barley straw mixed with clover, and one-third better than common fodder.

The cow or field pea of the Southern States is more like a bean than a pea, and is supposed to be a species of *dolichos* belonging to the pulse family whose species is undetermined. Be this as it may, its value as a farm crop has long been known. The ease with which it is cultivated, and its great value as a forage plant and as a fertilizer, have given it a prominent place in Southern agriculture. It belongs to the leguminous or pulse family, and is known as a pea, and for that reason it will be treated of under that head.

The letter below, from the Hon. H. M. Polk, of Hardeman county, is so thorough and exhaustive that nothing more need be said on the subject, only remarking that no soil in this State is so poor that it will not grow peas :

BOLIVAR, HARDEMAN COUNTY, TENN. }
July 2, 1878. }

Commissioner J. B. Killebrew :

I will not stop to demonstrate what is manifest to all that the South, from her sparse population, her widespread plantations, her adaptation to and her predilection for the cultivation of certain of our great Southern staples, is not at this time and may never be in a condition to keep up her arable lands by animal manures alone, and that her only alternative is in green crops turned under for renovating and increasing the productive capacity of her soil.

In estimating the relative manurial values of green crops to bring up the productive capacity of our soils, we measure by the amount of crop produced in the shortest time, the elements upon which these crops feed, their capacity for returning plant food to the earth, and especially by their leaving more or less of those elements in the soil which are necessary to the production of the succeeding crop. Nor do we omit to estimate their several capacities

for sending their roots deeply into the soil, thereby bringing up
and depositing near the surface the aliment for plants which would
otherwise remain below the reach of the roots of many of our most
valuable cereals. For the accomplishment of these purposes no
vegetable equals the Southern field pea and red clover. In them
we find the answer to that momentous question, how and through
what means can we, in the shortest space of time, bring our lands
up to their highest productive capacities to meet our own and the
varied wants of society. When we reflect that all progress, civili-
zation, refinement, culture, prosperity and happiness of society hang
suspended upon the scale which measures out the feeding capacity
of the earth, we begin to appreciate those vegetable productions
promotive of this desired end. The trefoils and legumes then begin to loom up in their grand possibilities; and the clover and the
field pea assume an importance not dreamed of before. Without
them, on the one hand we must descend to meager harvests, perish-
ing stock, fast approaching sterility, hard times and general discontent. On the other, by their powerful aid we ascend up to plentiful
harvests, fat stock, with the multiplied advantages resulting therefrom, good living, money in the purse, prosperity and contentment.
Can the pea and clover accomplish all this? Worked in proper
rotation with other crops they most assuredly can. In the heathen,
but appreciative past, when gratitude was manifested by the erection of temples, and by solemn worship to those deities from whom
temporal blessings were thought to flow, the pea and clover of the
present day have been entwined with the wheat and fruit, crowning
the brow of beneficent Ceres. Now, these mainsprings of successful agriculture in our favored land are but half appreciated, and
are thrust aside by the impatient tiller of the soil for some other
crop supposed to bring in more immediate money profits, but
which, in its continued drafts upon the fertility of the soil, must
end in the bankruptcy as well as the ruin of its possessor.

In a previous letter to you I stated some of the advantages which
the field pea possessed even over its great fellow-laborer, red clover,
as a fertilizer.

1. The pea will thrive upon land too poor to grow clover.

2. That it will produce a heavy and rich crop to be returned to
the soil in a shorter period than any vegetable fertilizer known.

3. That two crops can be produced on the same ground in one year, whereas it requires two years for clover to give a hay crop and good aftermath for turning under. In this time four crops of peas can be made.

4. That the pea feeds but lightly upon, and hence leaves largely in the soil those particular elements necessary to a succeeding grain crop, and the pea lay, in its decay, puts back largely into the soil those very elements required for a vigorous growth of the cereals.

5. There is no crop which is its equal for leaving the soil in the very best condition for a succeeding wheat crop.

6. It is the only crop raised in the South so rapid in its growth and perfection as to be made an intervening manurial crop between grain cut in the spring and grain sowed in the fall upon the same ground. And this alone makes the pea invaluable to Southern agriculture.

7. In our particular latitude it flourishes equally with clover, and with two such renovators of the soil (aside from their value as food crops), no portion of the earth is equally blessed. North of us the pea does not succeed; South, the clover fails.

8. Its adaptability to other crops, producing in the space between our corn rows both a provision and a fertilizing crop, with positive benefit to the growing corn.

9. The aid it gives in producing cheap beef, pork, milk and butter. Without the pea pork could not be produced cheaply where it costs so much to make corn.

10. A doubled capacity for wintering stock, and with this a doubly enlarged manure heap.

11. The large plantations of the South can only be restored by green crops turned under, united to a judicious system of rotation looking to feeding the soil. This must be aided by all the manure manufactured on the plantation.

12. The large addition made to humus, upon which the tilth, as well as capacity of the soil for retaining moisture, so greatly depends.

As for the cultivation of the pea, one can scarcely go amiss. When two crops are intended for renovating, break the land, sow broadcast and harrow in; or drill in rows three feet apart, and plow out when a few inches high. When the pods begin to ripen, if the crop is intended for manurial purposes, plow under with large two-horse plow, with a well-sharpened rolling coulter attached, or with chain passing from double tree to beam of the plow, to hold the vines down for facilitating covering. A roller passed over the vines before plowing under will assist the operation. Caustic lime should be sown upon the vines before plowing under to promote decay, and neutralize the large amount of vegetable acid covered into the soil. Select the pea which runs least. The vines are easiest covered into the soil. They are the black bunch pea, and the speckle or whippoorwill pea.

When planted in corn as a food crop, the bunch pea ripens soonest; but the Carolina cow pea, the clay pea, or the black stock pea are preferable, as they do not readily rot from wet weather, and will remain sound most of the winter. For early feeding of stock, plant whippoorwill pea by itself in separate enclosure from corn, where stock can be turned upon whenever desired.

Peas are often sowed upon the stubble after small grain is har-vested. Flush up the ground and sow either broadcast or drill in furrow opened with shovel plow, covering with scooter furrow on each side. Block off or run over lightly with harrow and board attached. Again, they are drilled in every fourth furrow, when turning over the stubble, the succeeding furrow covering the peas. When either of these last modes of planting is adopted, the peas should receive one good plowing out when they are from four to six inches high.

When planted in corn (the corn should have been drilled in rows five feet apart), they should be step-dropped in a furrow equally distant from each corn row, and covered with scooter with harrow or with block. This should be the last of May or in the first ten days of June. The only work they receive when planted in corn, is a shovel or sweep furrow run around them when the corn is being "laid by," unless there is much grass, when it becomes necessary to give them a light hoeing. The crop might be said to be made almost without work when planted with corn; in fact, it is often so made by those planters who sow peas broadcast in their corn, and cover them with the last plowing given the corn.

There is much diversity of opinion as to the proper treatment of the vines in curing them for winter hay. And as much has been written upon the subject, the writer feels some diffidence in giving his own views. Suffice it to say, the great end to be attained is to cure the vines to the extent only of getting rid of a part of the succulent moisture in the vine, without burning up the leaves. When exposed to too much heat, the leaves fall very readily from the stems and are lost.

When put up too green and too compactly they heat, and when fermentation of the juices in the vines, and unripe pods occur, the hay is seriously damaged, if not completely spoiled. Mildewed hay of any kind is but poor food for stock, and when eaten is only taken from necessity to ward off starvation. Some planters house their pea hay in open sheds, or loosely in barns, with rails so fixed as to prevent compacting. Others stack in the open air around poles, having limbs from two to four feet long to keep the mass of vines open to the air, and cover the top with grass.

There is diversity of opinion as to the proper manner of curing and preserving this hay, but there is none as to the value of this rich food for all stock, and especially for the milch cow in increasing the quantity and quality of her milk.

In attempting to renovate our soils by the aid of vegetable fertiltzers, we should not confine ourselves to one, but should utilize all which are suitable to our soil and climate. The writer has some sixty or seventy acres in clover, and in much of this grasses are sown. Orchard grass and Herd's grass thrive well with us, whilst blue grass and timothy find a congenial home in the lime lands of Middle Tennessee. In no part of the State does clover grow so well as in West Tennessee.

In considering the great advantages of the field pea to the agricultural interests of our people, I do not wish to be understood as disparaging other vegetable renovators of the soil. The field pea certainly possesses many advantages, such as its adaptability to almost any soil, and to many crops grown with it at the same time and with positive benefit to the crop grown with it on the same ground. Each row of corn should be flanked by a row of peas. Every spot of ground in the field too poor for corn can and will produce peas. There is nothing better to be sowed in old ploughed up broomsedge fields, and there, whilst the land is being fertilized, one of the best provision crops for stock, and the best of hay for milk cows in winter, is produced. And a still further advantage possessed by this valuable legume is its unequaled capacity for, and its unapproachable merit as an intervening crop, (being both a renovating and a food crop), between small grain or root crop in the spring and a grain crop in the fall. Do you ask more of any vegetable renovator? It is more valuable than the English turnip crop, and this crop, by those enlightened and eminently practical farmers, is estimated annually at millions of pounds sterling. It is doubtful if England could tide it over the next two years, if deprived of her turnip crop. It is the foundation of her stock and manure production. In contrasting the Southern field pea with the English turnip crop, we begin to perceive its immense value to Southern agriculture, and realize that too often, in reaching after the so-called money crops, we have neglected the best fertilizers (as well as food crop), ever given to the agricultural world.

In considering the present impoverished condition of the lands of the South, we are forced to confess it is the work of tillage—of injudicious, ruinous tillage. Where husbandry predominates over tillage, there is but little leaking out of the elements of fertility in a soil, and there is no estimating how long they will remain to supply the food necessary to a vigorous plant growth. The grasses, including clover and peas, are the grand elements for preserving and augmenting these elements in the soil. Hence we see all countries where husbandry prevails grow rich in soil, particularly if the tilled portion of the land is under a judicious system of rotation. Now, tillage, or the simple cultivation of land, puts nothing of any value in it, but is, of itself, a necessary *evil;* evil because of exposing the soil to a scorching sun, often reducing it to a mass of lifeless clods, and exposing it to an exhausting leaching process, which takes out its very life blood. The *cleaner* and *long continued* the culture, the more the injury to the land from the destruction of its humus, and from the greatest of all destructives, *leaching.* The injury is augmented as the land is rolling and broken. Hence cotton and tobacco (the first of which is not an exhauster of land, *per se*), have brought ruin to the best acres of the South, whilst small grain and the grasses have husbanded and increased the natural fertility of the lands of our Northern neighbors. Lands in which these too great staples are grown should be *level lands,* and in the case of tobacco should receive, (outside the aid of rotation), a generous manuring. But if I have given the true reason for the rapid decline of the productive capacity of the soil of the South as contrasted with that of the Northern States, let me take you one step further and show you that in the rich region of country lying northwest of the Ohio river, we find a very great difference in the material prosperity of the farmers there. A portion of them are prosperous, while others are experiencing all the evils resulting from the comprehensive term *hard times.* It is not difficult to learn the cause. The grain-maker, whose whole energies have been devoted to extracting the fertility of his soil for many consecutive years, in magnificent harvests, finds his crops growing less and less each year, while the stock-raiser is prosperous, having grown rich while making his land rich.

Time has here demonstrated a great truth which agriculturists should not ignore. Let our Southern farmers profit by its inevitable teaching. Let us determine to improve our destructive farming; give our lands a chance to grow better instead of depreciating yearly; build up the waste places; infuse new life into our Southern land, beautiful still in her decline, and endeared the more as we see her slowly sinking under the drain mercilessly kept open by her own children, in the veins through which her priceless life blood flows.

Since writing the above, I have accidentally found an old document upon "Southern Agricultural Exhaustion and its Remedy," from the able pen of the late Judge Ruffin, of Virginia. Although this article was not written specially upon the merits of the field pea as a renovator of worn lands, yet it shows its great value to the agriculture of the South so much more forcibly than anything I can say in advocating its claims, that I take the liberty of quoting the following paragraphs entire, and with them will close my letter, already too long :

" At the risk of uttering what may be deemed trite or superfluous to many, I beg leave to state concisely the fundamental laws, as I conceive them to be, of supply and exhaustion of fertilizing matters to soils and aliment to plants.

" All vegetable growth is supported, for a small part, by the alimentary principles in the soil, (or by what we understand as its fertility), and partly, and for much the larger portion, by matters supplied, either directly or indirectly, from the atmosphere. More than nine-tenths, usually, of the substance of every plant is composed of the same four elements, three of which—oxygen, nitrogen and carbon—compose the whole atmosphere; the fourth—hydrogen—is one of the constituent parts of water; and, also, as a part of the dissolved water, hydrogen is always present in the atmosphere, and in a great quantity. Thus, all these principal elements of plants are superabundant, and always surrounding every growing plant; and from the atmosphere (or through the water in the soil), very much the larger portion of these joint supplies is furnished to plants; and so it is of each particular element, except nitrogen, much the smallest ingredient, and yet the richest and most important of all organic manuring substances and of all plants. This, for the greater part, if not for all of its small share in plants, it seems, is not generally derived, even partially, from the air, though so abundant therein, but from the soil, or from organic manures given to the soil.

"But, though bountiful nature has offered these chief alimentary principles and ingredients of vegetable growth in as inexhaustible profusion as the atmosphere itself which they compose, still, their availability and beneficial use for plants are limited in some measure to man's labors and care to secure their benefits. Thus, for illustration, suppose the material of food for plants furnished by the atmosphere to be three-fourths of all received, and that one-fourth only of the growth of any crop is derived from the soil and its fertility; still, a strict proportion between the amount of supplies from these two different sources does not the less exist. If the cultivator's land at one time, from its natural or acquired fertility, affords to the growing crop alimentary principles of value to be designated as five, there will be added thereto other alimentary parts, equal to fifteen in value from the atmosphere. The crop will be made up of, and will contain, the whole of twenty parts, of which five only were derived from and served to reduce by so much the fertility of the soil. These proportions are stated merely for illustration, and, of course, are inaccurate; but the theory or principle is correct, and the law of fertilization and exhaustion thence deduced is as certainly sound. Then, upon these premises, there is taken from the land, for the support of the crop, but one-fourth

8

of the aliment derived from all sources for that purpose. And, if no other causes of destruction of fertility were in operation, one green or manuring crop (wholly given to the land, and wholly used as manure), would supply to the field as much alimentary or fertilizing matter as would be drawn thence by three other crops removed for consumption or sale. But in practice there are usually at work important agencies for destruction of fertility, besides the mere supply of aliment to growing crops. Such agencies are the washing off of soluble parts, and even the soil itself, by heavy rains; the hastening of the decomposition and waste of organic matter by frequent tillage processes and changes of exposure; and ploughing or other working of land when too wet, either from rain or want of drainage. Also, a cover of weeds left to rot on the surface, or any crop ploughed under, green or dry, as manure, is subject to more or less waste of its alimentary principles in the course of the ensuing decomposition. Therefore, it is nearer the facts that two years' crops or culture, for market or removal, would require one year's growth of some manuring crop to replace, and to maintain undiminished or increasing the productive power of the field. The poorest, and also the cheapest, of such manuring crops will be the natural or "volunteer" growth of weeds on lands cultivated, and not grazed; and the best of all will be furnished in the whole product of a broadcast sown and entire crop of your own most fertilizing and valuable field peas.

"Thus, of each manuring crop (as of all others), or of the fertilizing matter thus given to the land, the cultivator has contributed but five parts to the land, or its previous manuring, and the atmosphere has supplied fifteen parts. If, then, the cultivator, by still more increasing his own contributions, will give ten parts of alimentary matter to the land and crop, there will be added thereto from the atmosphere in the same three-fold proportion, or thirty parts, and the whole new productive power will be equal to forty. And if the soil is fitted by its natural constitution, or the artificial change induced by calcareous or other applications, to fix and retain this double supply of organic matter, the land will not only be made, but will remain of as much increased fertility, under the subsequent like course of receiving one year's product for manure for every two other crops removed. But, on the other hand, if more exhausting culture had been allowed, instead of either in-

creased or maintained production, or if the crops take away more
organic matter than nature's three-fold contributions will replace,
then a downward progress must begin, and will proceed, whether
slowly or quickly, to extreme poverty of the land, its profitless
cultivation and final abandonment. In this, the more usual case,
the cultivator's contributions of aliment (obtained from the soil,)
are reduced from the former value, designated as five, first to four,
and next successively to three, two, and finally less than one; and
nature keeps equal pace in reducing her proportional supplies from
fifteen first to twelve, and so on to nine and six, and less than three
parts. So the strongest inducement is offered to enrich, rather
than exhaust, the soil; for whatever amount of fertility the cultivator shall bestow, or whatever abstraction from a previous rate of
supply he shall make, either the gain or the loss will be tripled in
the account of supplies from the atmosphere furnished or withheld
by nature.

"In another and more practical point of view, the loss incurred
by exhausting may be plainly exhibited. According to my views,
soils supposed to be properly constituted as to mineral ingredients
do not demand, for the maintaining and increasing of their rate of
production, more than the resting, or the growth of two years in
every five, mainly to be left on the land as manure."

"These are the proportions of the five-field rotation, now extensively used on the most improving parts of Virginia. And one of
these two years the field is grazed, so that parts of its growth of
grass are consumed, instead of all remaining on the field for manure. To meet the same demands, the more Southern planter
might leave his field to be covered by its growth of weeds (or
natural grasses), one year, (and also to be grazed), and a broadcast
crop of pea-vines to be ploughed under in another, for every three
crops of grain and cotton. But the ready answer to this, (and I
have heard it many times), is, " what! lose two crops in every five
years? I cannot afford to lose even one." It may be that the
planter is so diligent and careful in collecting materials for prepared manure that he can extend a thin and poor application, and,
in the drills only, over nearly half his cotton field; and perhaps he
persuades himself that this application will obviate the necessity
for rest and manuring crops to the land.

"The result will not fulfill his expectation. But even if it could, the manuring thus given directly by the labor of the planter is more costly than if he would allow time and opportunity for nature to help to manure for him; whether alone, or still better if aided by preparing for and sowing the native pea, to the production of which your climate is so eminently favorable. All the accumulations of leaves raked from the poor pine forest, with the slight additional value which may be derived from the otherwise profitless maintenance of poor cattle, will supply less of food to plants, and at greater cost, than would be furnished by an unmixed growth of peas, all left to serve as manure."

"The native or Southern pea, (as it ought to be called), of such general and extensive culture in this and other Southern States, is the most valuable for manuring crops, and also offers peculiar and great advantages as a rotation crop. The seeds (in common with other peas and beans), are more nutritious, as food for man and beast, than any of the cereal grains. The other parts of the plant furnish the best and most palatable provender for beasts. They may be so well made in your climate, as a secondary growth under corn, that it is never allowed to be a primary crop, or to have entire possession of the land. It will grow well broadcast, and either in that way, or still better if tilled; and is of an admirable and cleansing growth. It is even better than clover as a preparing and manuring crop for wheat. In one or other of the various modes in which the pea crop may be produced, it may be made to suit well in a rotation with any other crops. Though for a long time I had believed in some of the great advantages of the pea-crop, and had even commenced its cultivation as a manuring crop, and on a large scale, it was not until I afterwards saw the culture, growth, and uses in South Carolina, that I learned to estimate its value properly, and perhaps more fully than is done by any who, in this State, avail themselves so largely of some of its benefits. Since, I have made this crop a most important member of my rotation, its culture, as a manuring crop has now become general in my neighborhood, and is rapidly extending to more distant places. If all the advantages offered by this crop were fully appreciated and availed of, the possession of this plant in your climate would be one of the greatest agricultural blessings of this and the more Southern States. For my individual share of this benefit, stinted as it is by our colder climate, I estimate it as adding, at least, one thousand bushels of wheat annually to my crop."

I can add nothing to what is said above.

I am, Colonel, very respectfully, yours, etc.

H. M. POLK.

Bolivar, Hardeman county, Tennessee.

CHINESE SUGAR CORN—(*Sorghum nigrum.*)

In 1854 some insignificant packages of seeds were sent from the then patent office, bearing this inscription :

"SUGAR MILLET.
(*Sorgho sucre.*)

(Good for fodder, green or dry, and for making sugar.")

Who could have foreseen, from these few characters, that a plant was then being added to this country more important than any since the discovery of America and the discovery to Europeans, of Indian corn?

In the midst of the great success of the New World in agricultural products, the Old World sent this boon to her offspring as a token of good will.

Within a year or two sugar has been made from it of good quality, and during a recent visit to the Agricultural Department at Washington, I saw specimens of sugar manufactured from a new variety as excellent in flavor and color as the best New Orleans sugar. I distributed some of the seeds of this new variety, and I confidently predict that Tennessee will, in ten years, make sugar enough for her own consumption at a cost less than five cents per pound.

HISTORY.

In the fall of 1853, Dr. Jay Browne was sent by the Department of Agriculture to Europe to gather seeds for distribution from the office. He saw a small patch of sorghum at Verrieres, near Paris, and being struck with its resemblance to corn, thought it would be an accession to our forage crops, and possibly might be used as a sugar plant.

Four years before, M. de Montigny had sent the seed from the north of China to the Geographical Society of Paris, in a package of many different kinds of seeds. They were planted, and but one single sorghum seed germinated. The product of this plant was distributed, and the next year, so great was the demand, a gardner of Paris sold his entire crop to Vilmoriu, Andrieux & Co., of Paris, for a franc a seed. Through them it was sent over the whole of Europe and America, for it was on their farm Mr. Browne saw it growing.

In 1850, Mr. Leonard Wray, of the East Indies, a practical sugar planter, on a visit to Kaffir-land, found the *imphee*, another species of sugar cane, growing around the huts of the natives, which they cultivated for its chewing qualities. On examination, he discovered its rich saccharine character, and was satisfied of its value. He therefore brought it with him to England and had it planted there, as well as in France and Belgium. He memorialized the French minister of war, and also Mr. Buchanan, who was minister in England at that time. He afterwards cultivated it in the West Indies, Brazil, the Mauritius, Australia, Turkey, Egypt and in this country.

The Kaffirs cultivated sixteen varieties that differed in the amount of saccharine principle, as well as in the time required to mature. In 1856 Mr. Wray exhibited sugar, molasses, alcohol, plants and seeds of the *imphee* at the Paris Exposition, and not only obtained a silver medal, but a grant of twenty-five hundred acres of land in Algiers was made him by the French Government that he might prosecute his researches. During this same year, Orange Judd, of New York, distributed 25,000 packages of seed to his subscribers, spreading them throughout the country. In 1857 Mr. Wray brought to the United States the seeds of several varieties of *imphee*. So then, when Mr. Browne obtained the seeds it was really in its initial state of cultivation in France. It had been grown in China from time immemorial, but with the exclusiveness of that people, its very existence had been jealously guarded from the world.

The same, or a similar plant had been cultivated in Europe at different periods during the dark ages, but the want of intercourse and the oppressive feudal system of that day had repressed any advancement in science and arts, as well as in agriculture.

The elder Pliny, in the first century, describes a plant under the name of *miltium quod ex India in Italium invectum nigro colors*, (a millet of dark color brought from India to Italy). *Millium* means thousands, and refers to the number of seed on a plant. Fuchius describes, in 1512, a plant cultivated in Belgium called *sorgi*. In 1552, Fragus says, in a work on botany, a *panicum plinii* was cultivated in Germany, and accurately describes this plant. In 1591, Gosner names this same plant *sorghum*. In Italy in 1595, in his commentaries on Dioscorides, Matthioli calls it *indicum millium*, or Indian millet. Gerard, an English writer, in 1597, describes this and other varieties of sorghum as dhouro corn, broom corn and chocolate corn.

Thus it is seen that this plant, however new to us, was cultivated in England, Belgium and Italy in the sixteenth century, and that it was known to Pliny in the first century. Its uses were described as so various that it is supposed all the varieties of sorghum were confounded by these different authors. It was recommended as fodder for stock, food for poultry and hogs, and for a syrup; while the Italians called it *melica* from its resemblance to honey. It was described as having seeds, various in color, from rufous to black, from white to yellow and red, and they were said to make an excellent bread. The bread had a pinkish tinge, being colored by the husks, which could not be entirely separated from the seed. Through the caravans of the Syrian desert, sorghum was carried from Asia to Africa, and there, under the changes of climate, soil and moisture, new varieties originated, and we have the *imphee* canes.

Linnæus calls it *holcus saccaratum*, and the dhouro corn he calls *holcus sorghum*. But Persoon, and others since, have separated the two, and applied to the sugar cane the general name sorghum, and its specific name nigrum from the color of its seeds. These plants are all called sorghum in the East Indies.

VARIETIES.

There are many varieties of cane, and while the description at the head of the article will give the generic characters, it will not the specific differences of the various kinds. But it is not necessary to give the botanic description of each variety.

FIRST RACE—EUSORGHUM.

True Chinese Sugar Cane, (already described).

SECOND RACE—IMPHEE.

1. Præcocia, (early Sorgo). 2. Oui-se-a-na, (Otaheitan). 3. White Imphee, (Nee-a-ga-na). 4. Black Imphee, (Nigerrima). 5. Red Imphee, (Cerasina, cherry red) Shlagoo-va. 6. Liberia, (Liberian).

In Tennessee the nomenclature is shortened by all being called "red" or "black," and "Chinese" or "African."

Sorghum, submitted to a pressure of ten tons, will yield about 60 per cent of juice, leaving 40 per cent of woody fibre, gum, juices, etc. Of this 60 per cent about 10 per cent is sugar, both cane and grape, or, if not reduced to sugar, it will make about 25 per cent of syrup, or 15 per cent of the expressed juice.

However, in fact, this amount varies very much, according to the soil on which it is raised. On rich bottom land, where the cane grows to be very tall and large, there is more water and less sugar in the juice, while on poor, sandy, dry land the proportion is much greater. In some specimens of syrup, when boiled down thick and allowed to stand, crystals of sugar will form all through it. These crystals are in the form of a modified rhombic prism. But in the generality of specimens, from the presence of an acid, the cane sugar is converted into glucose and no manipulation is sufficient to cause it to crystalize. A few years ago, at one of the expositions held in the city of Nashville, a jar of this sugar was on exhibition, and there is a fair specimen now in the cabinet of this Bureau, and, as before stated, some excellent specimens at Washington. Should an early and cheap means be devised to secure rapid crystalization the result will be to bring down the price of sugar. Molasses, which sold at one dollar per gallon, was brought, by the introduction of sorghum syrup, down to twenty-five and thirty cents. There is so little difference between this grape and cane sugar that it is to be hoped some process may yet be invented by which the syrup can be crystalized at will. The constituents are the same, only having one equivalent more ot hydrogen and oxygen than carbon. It is undoubtedly due to the presence of some acid, as cane sugar can be converted into glucose by the addition of acids, or by passing a stream of air through the boiling syrup. In this inventive age the mind of man has only to be turned to this subject and it will be done.

The Imphee cane, as a rule, produces more crystals in the syrup than the Chinese, consequently the latter is more universally cultivated, being better suited to making syrup. Besides, the African or Imphee cane grows much taller and is easily blown down by high winds, making a tangled mass in the field very difficult to harvest.

CULTIVATION AND HARVESTING.

Sorghum will grow and thrive, like dhouro, on the poorest soils. When the earth is parched up by drought it maintains its fresh, green color, and continues to grow. However, it will thrive better on rich land, and, though the juice may have more water, it will make far more syrup. The roots of sorghum penetrate the soil farther than any other cereal, and consequently deep plowing is absolutely requisite for a full crop. Not only should the plow, but the subsoiler should also be applied. On good land it grows to a height of fifteen or eighteen feet, on poor, badly prepared land it stops at five or six feet. Because it will grow on poorer land than other plants is no evidence that poor land is better for it. Therefore let the land be in good heat and the increased quantity of syrup will well repay the labor. On gravelly or sandy subsoils, the roots will go four or five feet deep, and on this kind of land, if rich, it will make far more syrup and of a better quality.

It should be planted in drills three feet apart, and in four or five days the young tender stalks will come up, looking very much like grass. But it will soon begin to grow rapidly, and outstrip grass or weeds. When three or four inches high it should be chopped and thinned out, and but little more work need be done to it. Two plowings are all it should receive, as the roots penetrate the ground so thickly the plant would receive more injury than benefit if plowed after it is three or four feet high. Besides, by that time the ground is so shaded by lateral branches and suckers the weeds will effect no material injury.

Much difference of opinion existed at first, and still exists, as to the best time of cutting. Some assert when the seeds are in the milky state, others when they are fully matured, is the most favorable time. A slight degree of frost does not injure it, and this opinion has caused the loss of many a crop, for, with our usual procrastination, this belief is allowed to influence many to let it stand until a severe frost comes, when the cane is rendered worthless. Whenever it freezes, fermentation ensues, and it will not make syrup at all, or, if it does, it is black and has a disagreeable odor. But repeated experiments have demonstrated the fact that early cut cane makes the best and cleanest molasses. Still, if the farmer has a large crop, he will have an opportunity of testing it in all stages, for it will take a long time to express the juice of a large crop and boil it down.

When the seeds are in the milky state, let the stripping and boiling begin. It is not our purpose to go into a lengthy detail of syrup making, it being rather our province to treat of sorghum as a cattle food than otherwise, and we will only give a general description. Besides, since the invention of cane mills and evaporators, there is hardly a man in the State who is not thoroughly conversant with the process. One thing every one should bear in mind, and that is, do not be too particular to press every particle of juice from the stalk. The first pressure, well applied, will get, generally speaking, all the saccharine principles, the second pressure only sending out gums, cellulose and some coloring matters. The syrup would be clearer and sweeter if the outer rind of the stalk could be stripped off and only the pith submitted to pressure. Let the juice be strained in a blanket, and boiled as rapidly as possible in a shallow pan. This is all that is requisite. Some use the continuous, some the interrupted pans. The former are becoming more generally used, that is, pans that receive the raw juice at one side and discharge the molasses at the other. Sometimes it happens that the syrup when boiled to a sufficent consistency does crystalize without any known cause. When it is discovered to do so, the farmer might take advantage of this accident and very easily make his own sugar. And to test its capacity to form crystals, a small quantity at various times of evaporating might be boiled to a point lower and thicker than for syrup and set aside to stand two, or four days. If crystals are thrown down in the vessel there is then reason to believe more of it will do so. He can, therefore, should he desire to make his own sugar, boil it to the proper consistency, or until the steam comes up through the syrup with a burst, and set it off in tubs to granulate. Sometimes, however, this does not take place for a few weeks, or even months. In order to expedite the process, it should be kept in a close, warm room, heated up to, at least, 90 degrees. This can be easily done by having the tubs or barrels of syrup in a room made tight, and heated by a stove. With but little replenishing of wood the stove may be kept hot continuously. When the granulation has taken place fully let the whole mass, molasses and all, be put into stout cloth bags and hung up to drain. Or it can be put into conical tin moulds, shaped like a sugar loaf, with an opening at the bottom covered by a wire sieve, such as is used for straining milk. The bags, however, are cheaper and equally as effective. Here let it remain for a sufficient number of days, to allow all the molasses to pass off. It can then be taken down and mixed with a very small quantity of water and redrained, and this application of water can be repeated until the sugar becomes as white as desired. The water can then be reduced by evaporation, to the desired consistency of molasses.

In the manufacture of the Southern cane sugar, lime-water, (white wash) is used to clarify it. At first this was used in sorghum but it was soon found that it blackened the syrup so much that no after treatment would restore its clear color. Besides, it gave it a a very disagreeable alkaline taste. Afterwards the white of eggs was used, which did very well, but further manufacture brought out the discovery that it contained so much gum it would coagulate and clarify itself better without the addition of anything with it. Skimming easily removes all impurities that arise upon the surface.

The amount of syrup procured from an acre of ground is as various as are the methods of cultivation and characters of the soil. From forty to two hundred gallons may be considered the range, and when it is considered that a cultivator can take his choice between the two quantities, it may seem that there is cause for emulation.

But it is rather as a forage crop that this plant properly belongs in this treatise. Its uses are almost as various as Indian corn itself. As has been already stated, it is greedily eaten in all stages by stock of every kind. The seeds are abundant, and one acre of good corn will make from forty to sixty bushels of seed. These can be cut from the corn and stored for use, taking care to spread the heads until they dry, when they make good food for cattle, horses, sheep, hogs and poultry. When ground into flour they make good bread. Both the seeds and the expressed juice have been extensively used in distillation, large quantities of alcohol and sorghum brandy being annually made from them. During the war it formed almost the only resource of the South for whisky, all grains being in too much demand for distillers to use them.

But probably it possesses more good qualities as a green soiling plant than any other one. Let it be sown either broadcast or thickly drilled with a seed drill very early in the spring, with about one bushel of seed to the acre, and there is no end to its feeding capacity. It will yield from twenty to thirty tons of green fodder to the acre, that, when dry, will make three or four tons of the sweetest and best of hay, and stock will eat up the last vestige of it. The proper time of cutting is when the heads begin to flower, when it can be cut and bundled as corn fodder, or left spread on the ground, if the weather is good, for several days, and it will dry enough to store, but not in too large a bulk. Its stems are so succulent that it will not cure quickly, the juices in it, however, will sugar directly, and then it will keep as well as timothy. It possesses fattening qualities in an eminent degree, and nothing like it was ever used for improving a drove of mules. But if the farmer has a drove of mules or herd of cattle or milch cows, it can be fed to them from the time it is two feet high, and they will eat it with avidity. By the time a field is gone over, it will be ready to cut again, as the root freely throws up new suckers, and will continue to do so until stopped by the frost. Thus, as many as three crops can be cut before it is destroyed by the cold. Or, if it is not wanted as green forage, it can be cut at blossoming, at least twice, without resowing, and the second crop will be as good as the first. A mule raiser in Williamson county has several large racks, and as soon as the hay is in condition to cut, he draws a load to each rack daily, and the mules are allowed to go to it *ad libitum*, so the farmer has only to give them grain to complete the process of fattening.

MANUFACTURE OF SUGAR FROM SORGHUM.

When sorghum was first introduced to the people of the United States they were informed it would not only make syrup, but that the Chinese made all their sugar from it. But little attention was given this product of cane however, and the cultivators were content to make it into syrup, as this alone made it of immense value to the country. Still every one who made syrup observed that occasionally it granulated so that it would not pour out of the barrel. In the face of this, writers set it down that the syrup was grape sugar and no treatment would make it granulate. This being accepted, no further effort was attempted to make sugar, and so the cultivation has continutd with that understanding until within the last few years.

The exception was established by the experiments of a few enterprising gentlemen who, reporting their success in eliminating sugar from the cane, were encouraged by the Commissioner of Agriculture, Gen. LeDuc, to extend their experiments until now it has been completely proved that it not only makes sugar, but to a degree that makes it very profitable.

This department being desirous of contributing everything in its power to add to the wealth and resources of the State of Tennessee, has made accurate investigations as to the process of sorghum sugar making in all its details. With this view the Commissioner has lately visited all the States engaged in the business and attended at the experimental works at Washington where the whole process was pointed out. In giving the details to the public the Department can vouch for the reliability of the statements in so far as the information of trustworthy men will permit. Of course there are the differences of climate and soil to be considered, but these will be in favor of the South, as we have decided advantages over the States North in the soil, which gives more saccharine matter, and in the increased time allowed for working the cane, from the length of our seasons. In this matter the department must acknowledge its obligations to Messrs. G. W. Stockwell and David C. Scales for valuable assistance. Before entering upon a description it may be of interest to say that in a short time one of the most enterprising business men of Nashville will engage in the business of sugar making. He is now getting up all the necessary information to enable him to go into the business intelligently, and there is no doubt but that his success will invite others to enjoy the profits of the business.

The process of sugar making involves an outlay of from $3,000 to $10,000, according to the character of the machinery employed. The former machine will not take the sugar through the refining process, only through the centrifugals, a machine that revolves with great rapidity and throws out the molasses, leaving a dry white sugar, equal to Coffee A sugar, but purer than any kind except the granulated sugars. There are so many adulterations of sugar, molasses and honey, that even were it carried no further, this would add greatly to its purity and healthfulness. Nearly all those beautiful fancy brands of syprus that attract the admiration of house keepers, are concocted from corn starch and poisonous acids, with the addition of glucose. Even much of our sugar is made from these materials, and it is impossible to eliminate all the poisonous acids from it.

The finer and more costly machines carry it through a refining process, making all the fancy brands of sugar and syrup. The establishment of a refinery involves the erection of numerous steam works to boil the syrup to the proper consistence, and these sell to the refiners their products, either in the form of syrup or semi-syrup and mush sugar. The latter is made by boiling the syrup to a certain consistence and then putting it in vats, where it remains in a cool atmosphere to granulate, which process is completed in forty-eight to fifty hours.

Cane is grown according to the directions given above. To make sugar, however, the soil is never fertilized, nor is the ground stirred after the cane gets twenty inches high, as either of these measures injures the character of the juice. The quantity of juice as well as its richness varies with every season. When the seasons are wet more juice is made, and when dry less juice but more sugar. In these there is but little difference, except in the labor of boiling down. In wet seasons the juice makes about 8 per cent of sugar, while in dry seasons it reaches from 12 to 14 per cent.

The best soil for growing sorghum is sandy or gravelly loam, and the land that makes nothing else will turn out a fair crop of the cane. It is the one crop that is unaffected by droughts; for let the season be as dry as it ever becomes in this country, the cane grows sufficiently large to produce a good yield. Cane stripped of its leaves will make from 37 to 39 per cent of its weight in juice.

An acre of first-class land will make 30 tons per acre, and it varies down to 10 tons with the character of soil and climate, and method of cultivation. The Commissioner of Agriculture at Washington caused analyses to be made of every species of cane grown in the United States, and ascertained that the variation in amount of syrup or sugar was so slight that but little attention need be given to the species. He also found out that it makes good syrup and sugar in every stage of its growth, from the milk stage of the seeds to their full ripening, so this peculiarity enables the farmer to begin the process of cutting and boiling down at an early period of its growth, which can be continued for at least six weeks after the full ripening of the seeds. He recommends, however, that it should be boiled down as soon after cutting as possible, as the juice in the ends ferments and some of it is thus lost.

The poorest syrup makes two to three pounds of sugar, while the best makes nine pounds per gallon. The medium and average may safely be put at six and a half pounds per gallon of syrup. But there is no loss in it, or not more than two per cent, as what is left makes a choice and superior syrup. It may be safely said that one gallon of syrup will make ninety-eight per cent of sugar and syrup.

In Minnesota, where the business has already assumed large proportions, there are but about two months in which to make syrup, while in Tennessee the seasons extend from the 1st of August to the 1st of January.

The refinery can work all the year from the store of syrup it lays in, provided the farmers grow enough to keep them at work.

The refinery in Minnesota buys cane and syrup. There is, as yet, but one large refinery, and that is at Faribault, Minnesota, although there are hundreds of lesser ones that act as feeders to the larger one.

From $2 to $3 per ton are paid for the cane, stripped and ready to grind, or from twenty to thirty cents per gallon for the syrup, according as the saccharometer declares the proportion of saccharine matter, which in every case undergoes this test. Thus the farmer is incited to produce a first-class syrup. By planting varieties of cane that mature at different times, the farmer can take advantage of the seasons, and thus get in a much larger crop, with less crowding for labor than if it all ripened at once.

From investigations made by Gen. Le Duo, there is but little difference in the amount of sugar or syrup between the Louisiana cane and sorghum, and it requires substantially the same machinery to convert it into sugar.

Dr. Wilhelm, of Minnesota, a celebrated chemist, has made discoveries of materials that free the juice of all acids and vegetable matters that have operated so far to make the taste of sorghum so objectionable to many persons. He and Messrs. Blakely, a capitalist, and Mr. Jolly, the inventor of the machines, have a manufactory of the machines, and they, in selling machines, agree to impart the secret of these chemical agents to purchasers, as well as to teach them the art of refining the sugar and syrup. By aid of these processes every grade of Louisiana sugar and syrup is made, and they compare most favorably with them. The polariscope shows a grade of ninety-five to ninety-eight per cent, the crystals are sharp and well defined, and the cubes are perfect, and this is all that is claimed for the best Louisiana sugar. The syrup will yield about seventy to eighty-five per cent of its bulk or weight in sugar. A ton of good cane will make one hundred pounds of sugar, and six gallons of syrup, according to the testimony of experts. If this be so, the profits of sugar making are enormous, as any one can see by a small calculation. The world has never yet had a supply equal to the demand, hence its high price. But if this business is pursued to its full capacity, the supply will stimulate a greater consumption, as any family man knows. In short, there is no danger of glutting the market. It may drive beets out of the trade, but it will always let the supply be as great as it may, command a remunerative price. The people of the United States every year send out one hundred millions of dollars to buy foreign sweets. The effect of keeping this immense sum at home, and distributing it among the farmers, will be felt materially. This economic view alone is a great inducement to this department to stimulate the production of sugar.

Nor is the production of sugar and syrup confined to sorghum.

Large quantities have been and are being made from Indian corn stalks. This department would not recommend the erection of machines for that purpose, but where they exist, and cane is stripped of its corn for roasting ears in market gardens, the stalks could be utilized in this manner rather than left to dry up. It does not make so much syrup or sugar as sorghum, but it is as good.

Capt. Blakeley has submitted specimens of sugar and syrup to the Merchants' Exchange of Minneapolis, and they speak of it in the highest terms as being equal in every respect to the sugar and syrup of commerce. It was then submitted to the polariscope, and it showed the presence of ninety-eight per cent of sucrose, or true sugar.

From repeated experiments made by the Minnesota refinery, and by the Commissioner of Agriculture at Washington, it costs about two cents to make a pound of sugar. Take the price of ten to twelve cents, its present value, and the profit is apparent.

Not only does this new process add sugar to the country, but pure syrup, a thing much rarer. Millions of gallons of adulterated honey are sold every year, as well as other impure syrups. By this refining process pure syrups of delightful flavor are made so cheaply they can undersell even the adulterations so common in all stores. The United States make 315,000,000 gallons of syrups from sorghum and Louisiana cane, while the country consumes twice that amount. It has its growth in the laboratories of the adulterator, instead of the sugar mills of the country. It will add no little to the healthfulness of the people when this vile trade is arrested, which can only be done by making a pure syrup that will undersell the fabricated article. Sorghum presents the only solution to this difficulty, and it is to be hoped the time is not far distant when it will be accomplished. It will require a large increase in the cultivation of cane. If the erection of mills has the same effect in Tennessee as it had in Minnesota, the increase in the amount grown will be enormous. It will be the same here, doubtless, as there are large amounts of land devoted to products that often fail, such as cotton, tobacco, and wheat. Sorghum never fails. When it gets a start it will grow with or without care.

The farmers of Minnesota grow early amber to the exclusion of all other varieties, and they think no other kind will succeed; but

9

Gen. Le Duc has established the fact that no material difference exists between them, one variety being as good as another. It may be well enough to try the early amber, however, and possibly the experience of Tennesseans may discover a difference. The amber is a sport or hybrid of some of the African varieties.

Above is stated the difference of the various machines. Supposing that only one refinery will be established, it will be of interest to farmers to know the best process of preparing cane for sale to the refinery. The ordinary mill and evaporating pan only are required. Let the syrup be boiled in the pans as usual, until it is of the ordinary thickness. In this form it is salable to the refinery as well as to consumers. At an outlay of $3,000 a farmer, or a combination of farmers can sell sugar to the refinery, or to the general market, that is equal to the best coffee sugars. This is done by the addition of a " centrifugal," an iron box with gauze wire sides, that revolves with amazing rapidity in a hollow cylinder, and it throws out every particle of fluid matter, retaining only the solid crystals of sugar. Of course, the centrifugal can only be revolved with the aid of steam. But steam is so far superior to furnaces for the evaporation of the juice of sorghum that it will be an improvement to employ it for that purpose even if a centrifugal is not provided. Hon. Seth H. Kinney, of Morristown, Minnesota, proposes to sell these machines and send a man to teach their use.

Another method of selling to the refinery is the " mush sugar." This is made by the use of the ordinary mill and evaporator and granulating pans. First boil the juice to a certain consistency, shown by an instrument called the saccharometer, then place the syrup in pans provided for the purpose, that shut up like a chest of drawers. It here remains for a certain time, varying from forty-eight hours to three weeks, when it is found to be in the condition that is called mush sugar, and it is then ready for the centrifugal or the refinery. It would be a good idea for several neighbors to pool together, and provide one centrifugal for a hundred mills, as it can be run at any time throughout the winter or the succeeding year.

These machines will soon appear, however, when the erection of a refinery creates a demand for their services.

Messrs. Stockell and Scales have kindly placed at the disposal of the Department of Agriculture a correspondence held with persons owning these supplemental machines, from which the following information has been gathered. The reader will notice how reticent they are about giving the details of the process they employ. It is the fear of competition which influences them to this silence.

W. Z. Haight, of Winnebago, writes:

" The early amber is the best variety for sugar making. Select sandy or gravelly land, and prepare it as for a crop of Indian corn. Sow the seed in drills four feet apart, and cultivate in the same manner as corn is cultivated. When the corn is twenty inches high allow it to take care of itself, as plowing it again would cut the surface roots, and thus injure the quality of the juice. When the seeds are in the dough state begin to cut, first stripping off the leaves and cutting off the heads. Cut it off at the first and last joint. Some allow it to lie after cutting five or six days, while others contend it is best to grind at once. I have never seen any difference, and the range gives more time to get it ground up. My syrup makes about eighty per cent of granulated sugar. It will make good syrup when the seeds are too green to germinate, and it also makes, for me, good syrup when it has been cut and has lain seven weeks. But this is an extreme that should be avoided if possible. If possible to avoid it, it should never lie longer than one week. An ordinary good mill and evaporating pan should make 20,000 gallons syrup in one season. I get my syrup worked into sugar on the shares, and my sugar will compare favorably with any sugar brought from New Orleans. Any farmer can reduce his juice to syrup, leave it in pans to granulate, and by use of a centrifugal convert it into sugar. The centrifugal is a sieve-like box that revolves with great rapidity, and it throws out the molasses, leaving the sugar. There is next to no waste in the syrup, as what does not make sugar will make fine syrup."

Mr. J. B. Thoms, of Crystal Lake, Illinois, writes:

" A ton of cane will make twenty gallons of good syrup. This syrup sells for fifty to sixty cents per gallon. Each ton of cane will make one hundred pounds of sugar and eight gallons of syrup. The machinery to work out one hundred tons per day will cost from $1,200 to $1,500. This includes the services of a man to teach the business."

Mr. C. F. Miller, of Dundas, Rice county, Minnesota, writes:

Cane machinery is very expensive. First-class machinery, with vacuum pans, centrifugal, bone dust filterers, etc., etc., will cost $10,000. This will work up a crop of two hundred acres in a season. A machine that will work up a crop of five hundred acres will cost double as much. But it can be used for refining purposes all the year. The business is more remunerative than anything I ever knew of. It will make any man of good judgment rich in a few years. He can make enough in the first season to pay all expenses, and the cost of the machinery. The amber cane is the best. It will make in this climate two hundred and fifty to three hundred gallons per acre. I have made four hundred gallons on one acre. Many other varieties are raised here, but amber is the best. The early orange comes off too late to suit us, but would make a fine successive crop with you in Tennessee."

Hon. Seth H. Kinney, of Morristown, Rice county, Minnesota, writes :

"About ten tons of cane is an average crop with us. The average yield is one hundred and sixty gallons per acre of good syrup, and this makes, on an average, six pounds of sugar per gallon, leaving the balance in syrup. It costs six and a half cents per gallon when made thick enough for sugar. We plant and cultivate in drills, as Indian corn is raised, rows three and a half feet apart. But I think it would be better to check it off on hills four feet apart each way. I strip the leaves off with a forked stick, cutting off the seed first. We prefer the amber variety. There are seventeen factories in my vicinity, each as large as mine, besides some smaller ones, all sprung up within the last two or three years. I have been grinding and making syrup twenty years, but have been making sugar about six years. I find it very profitable. I pay $2.80 per ton for cane. One ton makes one hundred pounds sugar and sixteen gallons syrup. I work at it five or six weeks. I have expended about $3,000 in perfecting my machinery. We have a good thing of it out here in Minnesota, and there is no good reason why you should not enjoy it also. It is within the reach of any man of ordinary intelligence. He can soon learn with a little showing. It is the very best agricultural pursuit we know or ever heard of. It beats wheat a long way with us, and will beat cotton with you. It is a cash business, also. It will bring in cash at all times, and never lacks a purchaser. It will pay you to send for a press and go into the business. I have made sugar now about six years, and each year find out something new that lessens the work and makes better sugar. The early amber is the best by all odds. I have supplied the Commissioner of Agriculture with amber seed every year for seventeen years. Last year I sold him 50,000 lbs. of seed, besides shipping 2,400 lbs. to Japan and 1,500 lbs. to France. It retails at fifty cents per pound, though I only got ten cents per pound. That I shipped I got eighteen cents for. The stalk of the amber is eleven to twelve feet high, and three-quarters to one inch in diameter.

This closes what is to be said on the subject. It is seen that there is a difference of opinion about the results or yield, but this arises from the difference in soil and treatment. But even taking a point far below the lowest estimate and it will be seen that the yield is very great. The man who takes the initiative in this business will probably work without competition for a few years. In that time he will reap rich rewards, for there is no doubt of the profitableness of this special industry. When the matter of making sorghum sugar was first agitated, this department held aloof from recommending it to the citizens of the State. It is the policy of the Bureau to act conservatively, and to do nothing and to recommend nothing that will cause the people to lose money. The attention of this Department has been drawn to it constantly by prominent gentlemen, among them the late Col. Sam D. Morgan, and now, by actual observation, it can conscientiously reccommend the production of sugar from sorghum as a highly profitable pursuit. And such being the conclusion, there is no good reason why our citizens shall not enjoy the benefits arising therefrom. Our State is peculiarly well suited to the culture of sorghum. The seasons are long, giving a sufficiency of time to work it up, and the reward is certainly stimulating. It is the opinion of the Department that more than one refinery should not be erected for the present, for it requires many small machines to keep one running. But there should be no limit to the others. More of the cane should be raised, and every one that raises it in sufficient quantity should provide himself with a mill and an evaporator. It would be a good idea for a number of men in each county to set up a centrifugal, and make sugar enough, at least, for home consumption.

Mr. E. S. Jones, of Pulaski, Tennessee, has met with considerable success in the manufacture of sugar. According to his experience the juice of the orange cane contains from 10° to 12° by Baume's instrument. This is from 2° to 4° sweeter than is obtained from any other variety of sorghum planted in Tennessee. The old varieties of sorghum require from eight to ten gallons of raw juice to make one gallon of syrup, while with the early amber and early orange it only requires from five to six gallons of juice to inspissate a gallon of syrup. This is a great advantage, as no more work is required to cultivate an acre of the one than of the other. Mr. Jones thinks the older varieties of sorghum have become impaired by hybridization with broom corn and other congenital plants.

The sugar which Mr. Jones makes is equal to Coffee A and C, and is free from the objectionable sorghum taste.

With the introduction of sorghum into Tennessee agriculture, it does seem that the last desideratum of the farmer is supplied. With a climate the most salubrious and equable, a soil the most various and comprehensive, it sends into the market, annually, grain and hay of every description. Her cattle and sheep are sent in large numbers into Northern cities, while her mules and horses supply the teams of the South. Fruits and vegetables anticipate the gardens of the North, and now she is able to draw a plant from Africa or Asia to supply her people with an ample quantity of home-made syrups and sugars.

BEGGARS' LICE.—(*Cynoglossum Morisoni.*)

Although this is nothing more than a weed, and a very trouble-some one when it comes in contact with sheep's wool, yet it per-forms a very important function in the economy of nature, as it constitutes one of the main dependencies for food in certain sec-tions of the State for stock. During the winter months the seeds adhere to the mouths of cattle, causing their mouths to look like warty excrescences adhering to them. The seeds are full of glutten and starch, and deer get fat on them in the season. This weed has seeds covered with minute hooks, so that they cling to anybody coming in contact with them, it being a provision of nature by which they are conveyed to distant points for germination.

It abounds in almost every section of the State, but especially on the " rim lands " in the " barrens," where it exists in the greatest abundance. Cattle are very fond of it, and it serves a useful pur-pose while all other food is destroyed by the cold weather. In fact, the cattle of the range keep in good thriving order on the seeds alone during the entire winter months. This weed, although it answers such a useful purpose as a food for both cattle and sheep, is a great pest, as the seeds render wool almost worthless, for they adhere with so much tenacity to wool it cannot be separated from them, and no machinery has yet been invented that can remove them. We would not recommend its propagation.

INDEX.

8050

www.ingramcontent.com/pod-product-compliance
Lightning Source LLC
Chambersburg PA
CBHW030607270326
41927CB00007B/1084